HALLMARKS OF CHRISTIAN CHARACTER

HALLMARKS
OF CHRISTIAN
CHARACTER

Peter Masters

THE WAKEMAN TRUST, LONDON

HALLMARKS OF CHRISTIAN CHARACTER
© Peter Masters, 2017

THE WAKEMAN TRUST
(Wakeman Trust is a UK Registered Charity)

UK Registered Office
38 Walcot Square
London SE11 4TZ

USA Office
300 Artino Drive
Oberlin, OH 44074-1263
Website: www.wakemantrust.org

ISBN 978 1 908919 80 9

Cover design by Andrew Owen

Printed by Stephens & George, Merthyr Tydfil, UK

Contents

1	The Clothing of Humility	7
2	Pursuing Positive Covetousness	21
3	Embracing the Pilgrim Concept	31
4	Sanctifying Power	45
5	Aspirations of Christian Service	53
6	Christian Mutual Helpfulness	65
7	The Defeat of Talebearing	83
8	Closeness to God	95
9	Spiritual Happiness	107
10	Walking in the Spirit	125

1
The Clothing of Humility

'Be clothed with humility: for God resisteth the proud, and giveth grace to the humble' *(1 Peter 5.5)*.

WHAT AN AMAZING EXHORTATION this is in these days of assertive self-confidence! Yet it is here we must begin this tour of hallmarks of Christian character. Clothe yourselves, says the apostle Peter, referring to the clothing of manual labour, as you would for some physical, menial task. Put on an overall, or some other protective clothing, and prepare for action. Humility, evidently, is a virtue which must be deliberately and consciously taken up. This passage is Peter's equivalent to Paul's Christian armour in *Ephesians 6*.

The clothing Peter has in mind is not merely a jacket or a hat, but something providing total protection, because we are vulnerable to different forms of pride – intellectual, spiritual, physical, and especially in our gifts and accomplishments. Humility is the only garment that can protect from the numerous arrows of pride. Do we make good judgements about different situations? If we do, the likelihood is we will become proud of this ability, and all too soon we will be exercising our own overrated human judgement on spiritual matters, rather than applying the principles of the Word. John Calvin remarked that 'everyone has in him the soul of a king,' and that is the trouble with pride. It creeps into us, and if we do not consciously resist it, we soon become ugly and repugnant in the sight of our Redeemer and Lord.

Pride has been described as being like weeds in a garden, kept at bay only by relentless hoeing and plucking. More than fifty years ago, my wife and I had two reception rooms in a house knocked into one, the central wall being solid brickwork. Everything was sealed up to protect the rest of the house against the dust, but you cannot keep brick dust from penetrating everywhere, and for weeks that dust continued to settle. Pride is like that. Once it 'erupts' it makes its way into every part of one's conscious being.

It is like a virus attacking your computer so that you need protective systems to keep it out, and these have to be revised constantly to maintain security. If we do not realise that pride attacks incessantly, and if we dream along with the idea that we can check our pride situation only occasionally, then we will certainly become deeply infected victims.

Spurgeon said that if the last enemy to be destroyed is death, the second to last will be pride. Of course, he was speaking imaginatively, but how penetrating, polluting, tenacious and destructive pride is! One of John Newton's devotional poems shows how pride (he calls it 'self') may wreck even zeal. Here are just three stanzas:–

> *Zeal is that pure and heavenly flame*
> *The fire of love supplies;*
> *While that which often bears the name*
> *Is self in a disguise.*

But self, however well-employed,
Has its own ends in view,
And says, as boasting Jehu cried,
'Come, see what I can do.'

Dear Lord, the idol 'self' dethrone,
And from our hearts remove;
And let no zeal by us be shown,
But that which springs from love.

When in a condition of pride many people readily talk about themselves, and even if their words are not blatantly boastful or self-preening, they nevertheless advertise themselves, whether by spoken word or (nowadays) by social media. Pride gets into every aspect of even the Christian life if we do not prayerfully don the clothing of humility. But do we know where to find this clothing or what we are looking for? It clearly can be done, with the Lord's help, otherwise we would not be commanded to do it.

Forgive the simplicity of this illustration, but we must open the wardrobe of the spiritual life, and as our eye ranges across the 'garments of humility' hanging there, we must select what is relevant to our immediate situation.

1. Think more of others than self

Firstly, humility – lowliness of mind – will think less of self and more of others *(Philippians 2.4)*. The humble spirit is less significant to itself. How do we become 'clothed with humility'? When we find ourselves thinking too much about ourselves and our concerns – whether in matters of well-being and comforts, leisure and pleasure, career and home, or whether feeling sorry for ourselves – we need to offer emergency prayer for help in switching off this whole train of thought and turning our minds to the circumstances and needs of others. Through prayer and desire, with the putting to death of self-centred thinking, and the conscious redirection of our minds to others, we put on the clothing of humility.

2. Cultivate a servant spirit

Secondly, humility, lowliness of mind, is open and ready to do anything for the Lord. It never recoils from any necessary task as if it is beneath one or an unreasonable demand. If something is advantageous to the cause of Christ, or will relieve distress, humility is always willing to do it. I remember hearing about a young man who had just secured his PhD in theology and been appointed as an assistant pastor. Within weeks of his appointment he sent a letter to the church leaders listing all the things that were beneath his dignity, such as putting out chairs for a youth meeting.

Humility thinks like a servant, firstly of the Lord and also of others. The model of Christian life in the New Testament is that of a bond-slave who is always looking out for the wishes of his master, and this is exactly our ideal attitude. Nothing is too much for a bondslave of Christ. Will we take up work in the Sunday School, teaching or collecting children, or setting up and clearing away? Or is it inconvenient because we like to rest, or read, or socialise? Everything we are and have should be at the disposal of our Lord, because humility is servanthood. Nothing which needs to be done for Christ should be too much trouble or too lowly, and putting on the clothing of humility means that we remind ourselves of this every day.

3. See our weaknesses

Thirdly, humility is always ready to see one's own shortcomings and weaknesses, and to try to improve. It is readily inclined to self-examination and self-assessment, and it is determined to learn. Humility values criticism and is ready to see relevant points even in hostile, unreasonable criticism, because its greatest concern is to please the Lord and advance the cause. It is willing to be shaped by circumstances or by people, especially husband or wife, and even by children. Prickly self-defence is a symptom of pride, whereas perception belongs to humility.

To put on the clothing of humility includes a frequent review of sins and faults of thought, word and deed, whether of commission or omission. Pride, by contrast, skims over self-examination, practising it only occasionally and superficially, but the baring of one's heart to God in daily repentance fosters a humility which is genuine and lasting.

4. Seek no recognition

Fourthly, humility is willing to go unrecognised, unthanked and unpraised for what it does, however unfair this may seem. As soon as the thought enters the mind: 'No one ever thanks me for what I do; I have received no acknowledgement or appreciation,' humility sweeps that thought aside, seeing every act of service as a privilege from the Lord. True humility bears no resentment. Moses was the meekest of men, who for most of his leadership of the Israelites received little apparent praise to sweeten or balance the undying unreasonableness of the people. The Saviour also endured almost constant hostility and ingratitude, and so did the apostle Paul. They were loved by some, but opposed and attacked by many more. Humility keeps no record of ingratitude and declines to think about it. So let us never lose a sense of privilege that we may serve the Lord and other people until the great day of undeserved rewards dawns.

5. Avoid unpleasantness and a critical spirit

Fifthly, humility is never discourteous, cold, abrasive or unkind toward other people, nor does it have a critical spirit. It is pride that returns evil for evil, and that cannot bear being offended or decried. It is pride that criticises and finds fault in everything but itself. To be clothed with humility is to adopt a determination to maintain a patient reaction to everything, remembering that we represent our Lord and Saviour in every situation.

The habit of readily criticising others is a particularly dangerous folly. The devil knows that if he can plant a critical spirit in us, our pride will be boosted even more than by flattery, riches or power. Criticism in the right spirit is surely needed to maintain the purity of doctrine and practice in the church, but an innate negative spirit is by its nature superior, arrogant, despising and self-blinding. For humility we need to tear from us any perpetual fault-finding tendency, including the subtle forms, such as a sense of humour which ridicules other people and their ways. To put on the clothing of humility means to adopt a positive, kindly, supportive, encouraging spirit whenever possible, never assuming the role of spiritual magistrate over others.

6. Maintain approachability

Sixthly, humility is never aloof, but approachable by others (*James 3.17*).* It will always accommodate others, never presenting a stiff, unsmiling, uncooperative 'front' to discourage conversation or fellowship. It will engage with both the youngest and the oldest believer, and embrace all sorts and nationalities. It has the spirit and disposition urged upon us in *James 2*, where the poor man is to be welcomed and respected just as the rich.

Humility is more than being approachable: it is being a good listener, willing and patient to hear others, their point of view, their ideas, their hopes, and their pains and woes. It is ready to hear out a person's case before making a response. Pride, by contrast, is hasty and impatient, always thinking it has something better to do than to listen, and if it imagines it knows the solution to other people's problems it will cut them short with its pronouncement before they have fully explained them.

Humility respects other people, especially fellow-believers, feeling it owes them helpfulness, remembering the immense debt it owes to help received from others.

---

* 'But the wisdom that is from above is first pure, then peaceable, gentle, and easy to be intreated, full of mercy and good fruits, without partiality, and without hypocrisy' (*James 3.17*).

7. Be uncomplaining

Seventhly, humility does not complain about its present lot in life (God's providence) but obeys the command: 'Be content with such things as ye have: for he hath said, I will never leave thee, nor forsake thee' *(Hebrews 13.5).*

Humility never forgets that believers have grace, life, spiritual understanding, communion with God, guidance, help, Heaven and every conceivable blessing, so that any hard circumstances that God has appointed in this world are far outweighed by the blessings. This does not mean that we should not strive to improve our earthly lot, or change a bad situation. But change should not be pursued as a proud quest for superiority and luxury. And if hard circumstances cannot be changed for the present, humility is willing to glorify God in them, and trust in him. Humility accepts God's will, and trusts his wise providence. Humility prays for relief, certainly, but until it comes, it trusts the Lord and submits to him. Humility remembers *2 Corinthians 12.7-10.* To put on the garment of humility is to shun unnecessary luxury in possessions or clothing, to avoid the cult of designer labels, and to pursue a reasonable lifestyle. (Nothing inflames pride like luxury and superior goods.) And the clothing of humility is donned when we suppress murmurings and complaints about our earthly portion.

8. Knowledge-seeking

Eighthly, humility always wants more knowledge of the Word. It takes a very realistic view of how little it already knows of the deep things of God, and pines for greater understanding and appreciation of God's being and ways, of how he deals with his people, of what he has in store for them, of his promises, of how life should be conducted, and of how problems may be solved from a right use of the Word. Humility looks for the daily reproof or encouragement of the Word, and for views of Christ, and for reminders of duties and privileges. It feels its need, fearing the consequences if personal devotions should be missed, and glorying in the syllabus of learning which lies ahead all the way to the end of life's journey. Humility looks up at a mountain of knowledge and stimulation for holiness, and feels its need of it. Humility commits itself to every gathering of the church for public ministry, allowing only unavoidable absences, realising that spiritual knowledge is not only cumulative, but a kind of consumable spiritual energy that must be renewed constantly by the study of the Word. Pride resents this concept because it likes to feel sufficient and equipped through its present accomplishments.

9. Thankful in all things

Ninthly, true humility thanks God constantly. How often do we complete a car journey in safety and step into our home without remembering that God should be thanked? Pride does not even think about it, assuming that all the credit is due to skilled driving, but humility knows that it is by the Lord's mercies we are not consumed, and thanks him for keeping grace.

Humility commits every journey to the Lord, indeed it commits every day to him. If this seems unreasonable, then pride has taken hold of us. Only pride finds it tiresome and excessive to depend upon the Lord for everything, but with humility it is second nature.

10. No mental fantasies

Our tenth characteristic of humility is that it does not construct mental fantasies or daydreams that place *self* on centre stage as the star performer in life. It does not write a script of self-exaltation. Many earnest believers will testify to having drifted into this kind of casual mental reflection when riding on a bus, walking, or doing some physical task leaving freedom to think. Then the mind has enjoyed creating its own 'soap', imagining some situation in which *self* is the outstanding person.

This is an acknowledged pastime for many young people, but

humility is not at all keen to be celebrated by this personal, inner fiction. It may seem harmless, but it is seldom humble, and humility is uncomfortable and keeps clear. Self-elevating daydreams or mental fantasies feed pride and involve putting *off* humility. To don the clothes of humility involves the rejecting of self-exaltation, and better control of one's 'thought agenda' in line with *Philippians 4.8*, avoiding the snare of vain imaginings.

11. View Christ much

Our final feature of humility is really the first and greatest. Humility makes much of Christ, standing amazed at him, and in deep admiration. Whenever his works and attributes are extolled in worship, humility truly marvels and praises him. In personal reading of Scripture, humility pauses at every view of Christ, reflects and reveres him. No sight of him is passed over lightly or taken for granted, so that our values and tastes are continuously primed and shaped by him, and we long to be like him, and conformed to his image. Paul states the principle in *2 Corinthians 3.18* – 'But we all, with open face beholding as in a glass the glory of the Lord, are changed into the same image from glory to glory, even as by the Spirit of the Lord.' To esteem Christ above all else, and to emulate him, is to put on the clothing of humility. While there was divine authority and power in the Lord when he walked on earth, there was revealed through his human nature the most remarkable and marvellous lowliness, seen in his kindness and approachability, in his acceptance of the mantle of poverty, in his uncomplaining patience, and in his tireless servant spirit. Never should we let slip our Redeemer as our supreme model and pattern.

Motivation to humility

Returning to the apostle Peter's words, we find powerful motivation to strive after humility – 'for God resisteth the proud, and giveth grace to the humble'. These are jolting words, and if we look at their context it becomes obvious that God resists not only the *unconverted* proud, but in corrective measure he resists the *converted* proud also. God will resist us if we allow the weeds of pride to choke humility. The word translated 'resists' means that God *stands against* us. Acting like a military commander, he sets his forces against the proud. The word suggests an advancing enemy that runs into an impassable barrier of soldiers deployed by a wise defending general. God does this to us if we are proud, and if we should try to break out to the left or to the right, seeking another route for our pride, God is ready to head us off and surround us so that we cannot move.

Our pride causes God to arrange himself against us, bringing us to a halt, so that every aspect of our spiritual life is impeded. He may cease teaching us as we study the Word, giving no rewarding insight, and imparting no comfort or pleasure. Guidance may also be withdrawn, and instrumentality almost certainly refused. How can we be used by God as his representatives while we harbour pride, which he hates? We may be called to a dead stop in every grace. Because we have indulged pride, the Lord may even deliver us over to our other great sins, whatever they may be. Perhaps our self-control will fail, so that we lose our temper and react proudly and testily to provocation. In the past, we may have kept up self-control, strengthened by prayer, but if pride brings about the termination of grace, then many falls occur. We had better humble ourselves early or the outcome will be very sad.

We have an insight into how God may 'resist' his people in a challenging verse in *Hebrews 12* (quoted from *Proverbs*) – 'My son, despise not thou the chastening of the Lord, nor faint when thou art rebuked of him.' We are warned not to despise the *gentler* punishments or chastisements of the Lord, because if we do there will eventually follow a more severe, testing rebuke.

We may think of the severe flooding in parts of Britain not so long ago. These are mysterious matters and we cannot comment on them too confidently, but such floods would appear to be a warning from the Lord, as described in the *Book of Revelation*, on account of the evil and unbelief of our society. But while distressing for many, what a gentle discipline it was, bearing in mind the absence of loss of life. Tragically, any possibility of spiritual warning was dismissed with contempt by our hardened society. So what will come next? If our land utterly refuses to contemplate any lessons that come from such troubles, or to recognise that we have a Creator to whom we must give account, when will the next level of chastisement come, and what form will it take? The gentler rebuke, if ignored, must be followed by a far greater one. Will it be soon? We cannot tell, because God, in his secret will, determines how long his patience will wait, but when punishment comes it will be very much harsher than the preliminary warning. Applying this to our individual lives, if God has taken measures to frustrate our pride, will we ignore him and wait for the much firmer discipline?

Amazing grace

Now we turn to an entirely positive and very surprising part of Peter's words: 'God resisteth the proud, and *giveth grace to the humble.*' It is only by God's help that we improve in humility, and yet he rewards us for that advance. The Lord is so gracious that any growth of humility attracts still more grace. This is an amazing principle rather like money making money. Humility makes humility. He gives 'grace to the humble'.

If we secure a measure of humility through prayer and 'putting on' the clothing or standards, God will give us yet more help in our spiritual lives – more power over sin, more answers to prayer, more blessed interventions in life, more deliverances, more help, greater usefulness, greater wisdom and discernment, more insight, more love, more gentleness, more benevolence, more faith and greater forbearance and patience. Will God give us more of these graces? Yes, if we pray for and work for humility, because his Word says he gives grace to the humble. He sets himself against pride, but increases the flow of grace which streams towards the lowly.

'Humble yourselves,' says Peter, 'under the mighty hand of God.' Humility is against every instinct of the corrupted human heart. A voice within tells us that it is not possible to live humbly, because we constantly need to assert ourselves, look after ourselves, struggle for dominance, and maintain our self-esteem. But, says Peter, we will see the feasibility and triumph of humility if we place ourselves under the mighty hand of God, believing that nothing is too hard for him, and whatever our circumstances we may rely on his help. If he calls us to go through deep waters, we will see that his providence is perfect. We will never need to abandon humility and adopt a self-assertive, bombastic spirit to power through life's trials.

Promised exaltation

The apostle next adds a great promise. We are to be humble – 'that he may exalt you in due time'. We may think that this chiefly refers to the end of life, as though Peter said, 'Hold on, whatever your difficulties, because at the end of life's journey he will exalt you.' But 'due time' means, in *the time appointed for you*, which could be very soon in life, and not just at the very end. At the right time, according to his perfect will, God will exalt us, lift us up, and bless us with instrumentality and joy, if we humble ourselves under his mighty hand.

Finally (still on the subject of humility), Peter says: 'casting all your care upon him; for he careth for you'. This means exactly what it says, but there is more. The word translated 'cast' is used elsewhere in the Greek New Testament, in *Luke 19.35* where we are told that garments were 'cast' upon the colt on which the Lord rode into Jerusalem, receiving the hosannas of the people. The original word means 'fling upon', as if an energetic act is in mind, showing that the people willingly, eagerly and decidedly yielded their outer garments for the service and recognition of the Lord. They did it for him as an act of approval and worship.

Here, also, in Peter's exhortation, the casting word does not mean that we wearily lay our troubles at Christ's feet for him to solve, although we may need to do that, but that we readily dedicate them to him as an act of service. We say, 'I will count all my burdens as my service for him, leading me to trust him, prove him, witness to him and draw near to him. I will certainly bring them before him to ask his help, but I am also giving them, offering them, to his service as part of my witness, and I must triumph in them through him. People must be able to think of me and say, "In all those trials he loved the Lord and proved him. He maintained his calm and humility."' If only we would do this the Gospel of grace would shine out of us in all circumstances, and people would be all the more touched, affected and impressed by the Gospel. Just as the people laid their clothes on the colt for Christ, we will give him all our trials as part of our service to him. And because Peter gives this exhortation in the context of humility we may draw the conclusion that counting trials as service to the Lord ministers humility to us.

John Wesley, prior to his conversion, went as a missionary to Georgia, proving painfully unsuccessful. In his manner and deportment he was obviously of upper-class stock, and very aware of it, often dealing haughtily with people of 'lesser breeding'. He behaved as an authoritative gentleman-scholar, but failure humbled him greatly. Back on the shores of Britain he began to call humbly upon the Lord, and only then could he become a leading instrument in the mighty Great Awakening that began in 1739. In due course he would translate the felicitous words of a German hymn –

Send down thy likeness from above,
And let this my adorning be;
Clothe me with wisdom, patience, love,
With lowliness and purity:
Than gold and pearls more precious far,
And brighter than the morning star.

George Whitefield, the most instrumental preacher of that awakening, was also prepared for his role by a gift of humility. The

Lord used circumstances and events to make him an immensely humble man, so that the Holy Spirit would convict vast numbers under his pleadings for souls.

It was the same with Martin Luther rather earlier. We tend to think of Luther as a strong, bold, self-assured person, especially when he nailed those 95 theses to the door of the castle church at Wittenberg, marking the beginning of the mighty Reformation. But Luther had become very humble before the Lord, knowing well that from that point on he would probably have no career in the church, no future as a lecturer in the University of Wittenberg, no approval, no promotion, and possible persecution and death. To obey his conscience would cost him all former aspirations and pretensions, and reduce him to a clerical outcast and rebel, but that was just the person the Lord required to be privileged with grace upon grace, and extraordinary instrumentality.

We see the same principle at work with C. H. Spurgeon. Considered naturally he was a brilliant man, but to prepare him for his life's work, the Lord denied him the means of a prestigious college education and brought him to a little, out-of-the-way backwater named Waterbeach, where he preached in a thatched church to cottagers, and took spiritual responsibility for a cluster of villages. There the Lord forged his instrument, giving grace to the humble.

If only we could all be more humble within ourselves. This does not mean that we should affect or pretend a form of humility in our outward manner, but that in our hearts and minds and in our relationships humility would reign. What grace would then be ours. Surely we should pray and work for it, watching out constantly for every tendency to pride and self-satisfaction.

'Be subject one to another, and be clothed with humility: for God resisteth the proud, and giveth grace to the humble. Humble yourselves therefore under the mighty hand of God, that he may exalt you in due time: casting all your care upon him; for he careth for you.'

2
Pursuing Positive Covetousness
What Christians Should Long For

'But . . . covetousness, let it not be once named among you, as becometh saints' *(Ephesians 5.3)*.

IT MAY SOUND surprising, but it is a fact that Adam and Eve were created 'covetous'. From the beginning, they longed for gratifying things, but in a good sense. They were made people of anticipation and desire; enjoyable sensations given in purity, when human nature was at its most refined. Of course, we were made to explore the Lord. We were made to drink in throughout eternity new sights, new understandings, and an ever-growing awareness of the wonderful being and ways of God. We were made for the everlasting exploration of his handiwork. The Garden of Eden was crowded with innumerable things to discover and enjoy, and our first parents walked that garden with hearts full of expectation. But then came the disastrous sin, and the fall from God's favour. The human heart became darkened and evil, with the love and longing for things still buried within, and those once-holy desires riveted themselves on earthly things. Since then, unfulfilled by the things of God, we have been at the mercy of fleshly appetites. The haunting couplet of Isaac Watts states the case:

> *Man has a soul of vast desires,*
> *And burns within with restless fires.*

This chapter, I hope, will not thunder against covetousness, pointing the finger, to make the reader feel wretched. It will reflect more the sympathy of the Lord, focusing on the personal harmfulness of sinful covetousness, and then on the benefits of *good* covetousness. We cannot get rid of *corrupted* covetousness unless we replace it with *good* longings and desires. The Scripture quoted at the beginning – *Ephesians 5.3* – shows both the seriousness of covetousness, and also the avoidability of it. We are surely encouraged to hear that it is a sin which may be conquered to the extent that it need not be *once* named among us. It should not be, and it is possible that it will not be, but only when this 'soul of vast desires' fixes its view on good and spiritual possessions.

We do not want to give the impression that nothing in this world may be appreciated. There are many, many things which we have been given to enjoy. We may legitimately desire, acquire, possess and enjoy, numerous earthly benefits. *Wrong* covetousness is when we want material things excessively or selfishly, as the following definition, drawn from several Bible words, shows.

It is fascinating to notice the literal sense of different Old Testament words denoting covetousness. One of them means simply to wish for, desire, or long for. It has the idea of fixing the eye upon a thing and dreaming of it. Another focuses more on the delight which is involved in covetousness. The first word highlights strength of desire, while the second supposes that we have now obtained that object of desire and proceed to revel in it, relish it, or gaze at it, deriving great pleasure from possessing it (especially if other people do not). We look at the object of delight, and are boosted in self-esteem and satisfaction.

Another Old Testament word could be translated 'love of gain', or love of more. To some people this is the engine of life. There is always something new to have. To stand still gives little satisfaction, and so new aspirations constantly ignite our restless minds. The lover of more comes to feel that he *deserves* more, and is *worthy* of more. Here is pure greed, acquiring ever-increasing things simply for the sake of having them. In this word, the covetous person is depicted as being driven by appetites.

A final and rare word describes a push for absolute security. We see here people who want to lift themselves above the calamities of life, and take steps to provide for themselves so well that they need never be anxious. In the Old Testament, certain rulers sought to place themselves beyond conquest or any other risk. Ordinary people also attempt this. This is not about making reasonable and legitimate provision for the future, but it is a fretful craving to be impregnable or undisturbable.

New Testament Greek coveting words are strikingly similar. There is one, however, which is different, and this adds to our concept of covetousness. It means *to stretch*. It speaks of the *effort* of reaching out to possess the desired thing. It shows covetousness to be a very costly passion, which dominates the mind and displaces concern for the things of God, for witness, and even for the pursuit of holiness. Most of the offender's emotional energy becomes focused on getting or attaining an earthly objective. This comes first. Another New Testament word means *to set the heart on*. Another means *to desire more*. Yet another is to be *fond of silver* or of money, and all that it can buy. Such words together provide a comprehensive definition of covetousness. They cover the *thinking* element, including the initial desiring and growing longings. They show the cost of acquiring things, and the nourishing of satisfaction by gloating and relishing. They include even the passion for absolute security. 'Beware of covetousness,' says the Lord, in the Parable of the Rich Fool. It is to be feared. Here are some reasons why.

First, covetousness is intensely damaging to believers because it is *carnal, animal and earthly*. It is all to do with the Fall. It is fleshly. When covetousness takes over we become focused on earthly goods or attainments. Covetousness is the passion of the unsaved, and God will not have it admitted to Heaven. Paul says – 'For this ye know, that no … *covetous man* … hath any inheritance in the kingdom of Christ and of God.' Apart from its offensiveness to God, it overturns the sensitive equipment of the believer's soul, dragging it away from spiritual concerns and back to earthly ones.

Secondly, covetousness will damage believers because it is *an act of worship*. In *Ephesians 5.5* it is described as a form of idolatry. It is an act of worship in which we depend upon worldly sources of relief, comfort, satisfaction, pleasure and emotional uplifting instead of divine benefits. It is the switching of devotion from God to earth. 'Let your conversation be without covetousness,' says the writer of *Hebrews*, 'and be content with such things as ye have: for he hath said, I will never leave thee, nor forsake thee.' There is an unmistakable 'either-or' nestling in this verse. 'If you are covetous,' says the Lord in effect, 'you cannot seek your pleasures from me. You have committed idolatry. You have chosen to worship at this world's shrine, rather than at the true shrine.' In *Luke 16* the Lord says, 'No servant can serve two masters.' The alternatives are God or mammon.

Thirdly, covetousness undoubtedly *dulls and anaesthetises* all our spiritual aims, tastes and values. The more covetous we are, the less we desire and enjoy spiritual blessings. Filling our hearts with earthly things, covetousness makes us skip our devotional reading and lose fervour and commitment in our prayers. If we are engaged in service for the Lord, we soon begin to take shortcuts. We prepare less thoughtfully and lovingly our lessons and visual aids, or what-ever we do. In *Psalm 119.36* the psalmist says – 'Incline my heart unto thy testimonies, and not to covetousness.' It is one or the other. Either we yearn for spiritual advance, or for material gain. It cannot be both. The apostle Paul makes the same point in *Colossians 3.2*: 'Set your affection on things above, not on things on the earth.'

Fourthly, covetousness *severs our communion* with God. In *Isaiah 57.17* God says, 'For the iniquity of his covetousness was I wroth, and...I hid me.' If I am covetous, even momentarily, God hides from me. He will not smile on me. I will not be assured; I will not have his blessing so wonderfully poured down upon me.

Fifthly, covetousness is to be feared because it eventually *takes a believer over*. *Proverbs 21* tells us of a poor man who nevertheless 'coveteth greedily all the day'. In other words he becomes obsessed with the object of his desire. Perhaps the most famous passage containing the coveting word is *1 Timothy 6.10* – 'For the love of money is the root of all evil: which while some coveted after, they have erred from the faith, and pierced themselves through with many sorrows.' Paul is speaking about Christians who so toyed with covetousness they became greatly backslidden and denied the faith. No doubt, if truly saved, God would have chastened them and brought them back, but not without many sorrows. Covetousness can get such a hold on us that it exceeds our power to control it.

Sixthly, covetousness is to be feared because it is probably *the most stealthy of all sins*. When Paul seeks an example of how the law is needed to point out sin, he chooses covetousness. 'I had not known lust,' he says, 'except the law had said, Thou shalt not covet' *(Romans 7.7)*. Covetousness is so crafty and so gradual in its influence that the law must awaken us to it. Though we set our minds on earthly things wilfully, our desire snowballs, and we do not see where we are heading. Here is an unrecognised sin, only to be detected by firm self-examination. What am I after? What am I daydreaming about? What is swamping my desires?

Seventhly, covetousness is to be avoided because it is such *an infectious sin*. Our sin will so easily ruin others, even our children. This is why (along with other sins) Paul commands that we keep no company with a covetous person. 'If any man that is called a brother,' he says, be 'covetous ... with such an one no not to eat.' It is one of the excommunicable sins partly because it is so infectious.

Eighthly, covetousness is to be torn away from our hearts because it *disqualifies from leadership roles* in the church of Christ. When Moses was instructed how to appoint leaders in his day, he was told that they must be those 'hating covetousness' *(Exodus 18.21)*. Yet we know of churches which appoint rich-living men in the belief that this is a mark of achievement and capability. One of the essential qualifications of office bearers mentioned in *1 Timothy 3.3* is that they are 'not covetous'. Paul says to the elders of the church at Ephesus – 'I have coveted no man's silver, or gold.' Covetousness grieves the Holy Spirit and thereby ruins Christian service. It is essential that we avoid it.

Ninthly, covetousness is to be avoided because it *fuels self-reliance*, and a spirit not willing to accept the providence of God. *Habakkuk 2.9* reads – 'Woe to him that coveteth an evil covetousness to his house, that he may set his nest on high, that he may be delivered from the power of evil!' (*Evil* here means calamity.) We have already noted this form of covetousness. It describes a person who loves his money and earthly possessions so much he must ensure that he will never allow them to be eroded or diminished. He does not want to think that anything could pull him down, and goes beyond reasonable provision. He cannot rest in the hands of God, and trust him.

To summarise, covetousness is a craving for something for ourselves. It is revelling in that thing and drawing satisfaction from it. It is pride in the possession of the thing. It is always wanting more. It is placing an object of desire before the love and service of the living God. It is striving for absolute self-provision and security. These are the monster's several heads, and the object (or objects) of interest may be material possessions, substance, pleasures, honours, applause, admirers, influence or power.

How may we avoid covetousness? Here are a few sentences of direct advice. Do not daydream about possessing earthly things. Do not dwell on them overmuch. If you have to weigh options in making a decision, ration your thoughts. Never let a decision about a material acquisition occupy your attention morning, noon and night, savouring every moment, for you will be hijacked by the coveting process. Do not justify things that you know you do not really need. And don't excuse the coveting of small things simply because they are small items, for you will be weakened, and the coveting process will reach out for bigger objectives.

The best way to avoid wrong longings is to indulge in *positive* covetousness. We need to switch our commitment and desire to better things, training ourselves to covet *well.*

We should, for example, covet *souls and instrumentality* for the Lord, longing to have these. With Paul we must say – 'Brethren, my heart's desire and prayer to God for Israel is, that they might be saved' *(Romans 10.1).* We must long more for the souls of our relatives and work colleagues, often asking ourselves – 'What can I do; what can I contribute; to whom can I speak, in order to reach souls?' We should take responsibility for selected people in regular prayer, for this is the covetousness that God loves and rewards.

Then again we need to covet *holiness,* being commanded in *Hebrews 12.14* to 'follow *[pursue or strive after]*...holiness'. Our positive coveting should cause us to long in the week before us to have greater Christian character, to be a better, deeper, stronger and more self-controlled person.

Another positive and priceless object of good covetousness is to possess more of the love of Christ toward others. Paul exhorts in *Philippians 2.4* saying, 'Look not every man on his own things, but every man also on the things of others.' If only we could learn to long for the spiritual advance, health, well-being and happiness of others! There are so many people whose needs we know well, but are we helping them in any way? When our minds become fixed on something for *ourselves*, perhaps something yet more for *our* home, for *our* life, we must repent, and pray for help to switch off those thoughts, and desire good for others, especially those of the household of faith.

Yet another legitimate 'lust' is to have the skill and opportunity to edify others. Does not Paul say, 'seek that ye may excel to the edifying of the church'? (The word 'seek' is a strong coveting word.) This is said in the context of certain spiritual gifts given at that time, but the principle is for all believers in all ages. Paul exhorts us only to speak that 'which is good to the use of edifying, that it may minister grace unto the hearers' *(Ephesians 4.29)*. We must ask ourselves what our conversation is like, and whether we contribute to the edifying and building up of the church. What a noble desire it is to long for this!

Higher than any desire for adventure and discovery in this world is the longing for greater experience in proving the Lord in daily life. The daily asking and receiving of the Christian walk is gloriously enshrined in passages such as *Ephesians 6.18* – 'Praying always with all prayer and supplication in the Spirit, and watching thereunto with all perseverance.' Says the Saviour: 'Ask, and it shall be given you; seek, and ye shall find; knock, and it shall be opened unto you: for every one that asketh receiveth; and he that seeketh findeth; and to him that knocketh it shall be opened' *(Matthew 7.7-8)*. And James warned: 'Ye have not, because ye ask not.' Here lies so much of our assurance and thanksgiving, and surely it is a worthy object of positive, edifying covetousness.

Then we may covet the gift of wisdom, desired for all believers by Paul in *Philippians 1.8-9* – 'How greatly I long after you all…that your love may abound yet more and more in knowledge and in all judgment *[or discernment]*.' We should long to have this first for ourselves, and then for other, especially young, believers. Some are fragile, so let us covet their safety with great longing, and desire that the Lord will give them deep spiritual insight in these perilous times.

Obviously it is good covetousness to long for Heaven. In a remarkable text Paul says, 'For I am in a strait betwixt two, having a desire *[a tremendous longing]* to depart, and to be with Christ' *(Philippians 1.23)*. This is a desire which should deepen in passion as we grow in grace. We should long for Heaven more than anything in this life; anything less is an insult to the Lord. Says Paul, 'Reaching forth unto those things which are before, I press toward the mark for the prize of the high calling of God in Christ Jesus' *(Philippians 3.13-14)*. He wanted future things, and so must we, building up our anticipation and longing.

It is a most noble longing or coveting to desire peace with others. 'Let him seek peace, and ensue it,' says Peter *(1 Peter 3.11)*, using a coveting verb. Let believers long for peace, for they bear the likeness of the supreme Peacemaker. If there is tension between ourselves and another believer, we should long for harmony to be restored, never nursing hurts or offences. We should covet also the gift of being bridge-builders who spread peace, realising it is not enough to accept the desirability of this, but to long for it.

Good coveting must also include a longing for fellowship. It is said of Epaphroditus that he longed after the Philippian believers, pining for their fellowship. Of course, legitimate desire for fellowship goes beyond the pleasure of friendship. It includes sharing the things of God; it is a desire to share in spiritual succour and service.

Highest of all among things to be desired or coveted should be the pleasing of our Saviour and Lord. Paul complains that – 'all seek their own, not the things which are Jesus Christ's' *(Philippians 2.21)*. The supreme way to exclude bad covetousness is to long for the interests of Jesus our Lord above all else. If we only daydreamed about his work we would be delivered from so many fleshly, earthly lusts. Let us be those people who pine for the success of the work of the Gospel, and who enjoy reading about it, hearing about it, and talking about it.

In conclusion, it is vital to ration our thoughts when it comes to earthly things, and then to divert our thoughts from the corrupt forms of coveting to the good. Let us set for ourselves new objectives in desiring, then the crippling temptations of bad desire will be beaten down, and will recede into the background. We are beings of anticipation and desire, but these must be applied to godly objectives where they will reap immeasurable pleasure and satisfaction according to God's gracious purpose.

A challenging hymn of Augustus Montague Toplady is an ideal prayer for good covetousness:–

> *Emptied of earth I long to be,*
> *Of sin, of self, and all but thee;*
> *Wholly reserved for Christ that died,*
> *Surrendered to the Crucified:*
>
> *Withdrawn from all the noise and strife,*
> *The lust, the pomp and pride of life;*
> *For Heaven alone my heart prepare,*
> *And have my conversation there.*
>
> *Nothing, save Jesus, would I know;*
> *My friend and my companion thou!*
> *Lord, seize my heart, assert thy right,*
> *And put all other loves to flight.*
>
> *All idols – tread beneath thy feet,*
> *And to thyself the conquest get:*
> *Let sin no more oppose my Lord,*
> *Slain by the Spirit's two-edged sword.*
>
> *Greater communion let me prove*
> *With thee, blest object of my love;*
> *But O, for this no power have I;*
> *My strength is at thy feet to lie.*

3
Embracing the Pilgrim Concept

'These all died in faith, not having received the promises, but having seen them afar off, and were persuaded of them, and embraced them, and confessed that they were strangers and pilgrims on the earth'
(Hebrews 11.13).

THE BIBLE is full of pilgrimage. The eleventh chapter of *Hebrews* speaks among others of Abel, Enoch, Noah, Abraham, Isaac and Jacob, who are described as 'strangers and pilgrims on the earth'.

'Strangers' literally means foreigners, people of a different culture and language. 'Pilgrims' are those who are living in a foreign land, away from their own people. In the Bible the pilgrim word implies a journey – travelling home – as we see in *Hebrews 11.14*. It describes those who 'seek a country'. Biblical pilgrims live in another country, alongside the resident community, but they do not fully integrate. They are 'alongsiders', soon to go home. They may accomplish great things for the benefit of the country in which they live (as Joseph did), but they never cease to be pilgrims.

They are not like expatriates who choose to settle in another country either because they are making their career there, or because they like it better than their own country. Most 'expats' are where they are because they want to be, but a sojourner or pilgrim in the Bible has no burning desire to be where he is, except for the service of the Lord, the salvation of souls, and the love of his family. A pilgrim's primary interest is not in his present country. The concept of pilgrimage is tremendously important to the Christian, giving guidance on the believer's stance in all circumstances of life. Without this concept we become reabsorbed into the life and culture of this fallen world, and also unnecessarily sensitive to all the problems and trials of this worldly life.

The pilgrim concept is specially vital at the present time, when an increasing number of evangelicals advocate being 'culturally progressive' or 'culturally relevant', exhorting us to get much more into the world. The very word 'pilgrim' sounds a warning, reminding us of our duty to be distinctive and set apart for Christ.

That most famous book, John Bunyan's *The Pilgrim's Progress*, powerfully takes up the pilgrim term. We remember, too, how Jacob spoke of 'the days of the years of my pilgrimage', and that David said, 'I am a stranger with thee, and a sojourner, as all my fathers were' *(Psalm 39.12)*. He was a king over his people, and yet he declared himself to be a foreigner and a temporary resident. The apostle Peter also referred to believers as 'strangers and pilgrims'. Is this term true of us?

The heroes of faith in *Hebrews 11* – 'all died in faith, not having received the promises *[in their earthly lifetime]*, but having seen them afar off, and were persuaded of them, and embraced them'. They made the promises of an eternal home the inspiration and engine of their lives, declaring by their lifestyle that they were strangers and pilgrims on the earth. Their lives said, 'We do not belong here. We are foreigners and temporary dwellers, living in tents, and looking forward to something far better.'

Today's new teaching says we must love it here, do the things that worldings do, sing their songs, play their genre of music, watch their films and plays, dance their dances, and wear their most daring styles, along with other compromises that would have horrified believers throughout the last two millennia.

Sometimes we see television news pictures of people in wealthy countries who have suffered storm damage to homes and possessions (we are not referring to the more terrible catastrophes including loss of life). No doubt most of the people are insured and will survive, obtaining new homes and goods, but they are seen distraught and inconsolable, as if their world has come to an end. We understand the shock and upheaval, and the disappointment of losing appreciated things, but so often we see a reaction more appropriate for lives being lost. It has evidently meant too much to the sufferers to lose the things they possessed. What has happened seems to them the greatest blow imaginable. In the past, Bible pilgrims never thought like that. This world was never their place. Earthly losses and disappointments were never the end of the world to them, because their minds and hearts were not set wholly on earthly things. In a sense they travelled lightly through life, and so should we.

There were three pilgrim feasts in the Old Testament, when the people would go to Jerusalem. There was the Passover, which commemorated the deliverance from Egypt. Pentecost commemorated the end of the grain harvest. The Feast of Tabernacles marked the end of the agricultural working year, also recalling the wilderness journeyings. All these feasts involved pilgrimage, which reminded the people that all of life is a pilgrimage. On the journey they sang the pilgrim psalms, or songs of degrees (*Psalms 120-134*), especially during the final ascent to the city. The pilgrim theme was a major feature of the calendar.

Are we prepared for a pilgrimage, or do we expect fulfilment and purpose from this alien land? As foreigners, we should take every opportunity to make the world a better, kinder, fairer place to live in, but it is not our place, and many worldly people resent us, or are fairly cool toward us. It is heresy to think that Christ's purpose is the social reformation of the world. Good works of compassion and aid are part of our witness, but the clear biblical view of the world is that it is a fallen and doomed world, from which Christ is gathering out his people by grace.

We no longer think like worldlings, or have the same aspirations, or enjoy the same things. We are bound to be suspected, misunderstood, and even hated. Though many people may be respectful toward us, and appreciative, many more will be hostile in some degree. All believers at some time experience some form of persecution, and for many it will be very bitter. If we don't understand this, then it will be very painful to us. We should try to be as engaging as we can be, and as helpful and courteous, but we so often remain misfits as far as this world is concerned.

If we know what it means to be pilgrims for Christ, then we understand this, and derive our happiness and peace from him alone. We expect to be slandered and unfairly treated by the world. Not only is the world hostile to us, but also the devil. He often takes advantage of us while we are 'on the road' away from home, firing at us temptation, despondency, and even doubts of our standing with the Lord. But we are provided with many helps and blessings on our pilgrim way to balance these things.

Six benefits from Christ

Whatever the trials of pilgrimage, we must set against them the overwhelming benefits, the best of which are described by the Saviour in his great high priestly prayer in *John 17*. We are the enlightened ones, the knowing ones (v 8), those who belong to God (v 10), people who will certainly be kept (v 11) and never lost (v 12), who will have certain joy (v 13), who are sent into the world on a divine mission (v 18), who will be sanctified (v 19), whose mission will succeed (v 20), who will ultimately be vindicated (v 23), and who will finally see the glory of the Lord (v 24).

1. Benefit of fellowship

The benefits shine out from *Hebrews 11.13* also – 'These all died in faith, not having received the promises, but having seen them afar off.' We particularly notice the word 'all', which reminds us that there are countless believers. We are not alone; there are many others.

It is so precious and valuable for believers to join together on the Lord's Day and at weeknight gatherings to hear the Word, to fellowship together, and to draw pleasure and solace from each other. It is sad when Christians don't know many people in their church fellowship, because one of the greatest comforts in the life of a pilgrim is that there are many of us in this family.

Round the world there are millions and millions of Christ's people. Of course we cannot know all of them, but we may think of others, even in the most isolated places. Countless people love Christ and his Word, and live as pilgrims passing through this present evil world. There are far more than we realise, even in our land, and certainly throughout the world. Vast is the company of those who have been brought to see through this world, have met with Christ, and now walk with him. We are not talking about a few pilgrims, but about the largest nationality or clan of like-minded people on earth.

2. Benefit of experience

Another benefit that engages our attention in *Hebrews 11.13* is the fact that our pilgrimage is a very well-proven journey. The phrase – 'These all died *in faith*' – extends from the first generation of people on earth to the twenty-first century. Millions of saved people have taken this journey before us, and have proved the Lord. We see a portrayal of this vast scheme set out in the Scriptures. Here are the histories of those who have proved him through mighty deliverances. They were vindicated and blessed, finishing their journey in triumph and happiness. So have a great throng down the rolling centuries since. How moving it is to read the biographical accounts of the people of faith, including the famous proclaimers, who adorn history! The encouragements and lessons are innumerable. This is a well-trafficked and well-proven journey, and we are not by any means the pioneers.

3. Benefit of security

Allied to this we see in *Hebrews 11.13* the doctrine of the perseverance of the saints, for *all* the pilgrims 'died in faith', kept safely to the end by the power of God, in spite of their own weaknesses and inadequacies. If they fell into some foolish pitfall by their own sinfulness, even if the Lord had to discipline them, he rescued them from that fall, and they were restored to the full joy of their salvation. Every twist and turn of the pilgrim journey is known to God, who watches every step of his people. No man and no force in earth or hell can pluck them out of his hand.

Believers never forget that they are on their way to that place where there is no more death, sin, pain, or suffering, and even now they have the 'earnest' of their inheritance, the 'down payment' as it were, their new nature, new understanding and their spiritual faculties and joys.

4. Benefit of the Spirit

Can there be any greater privilege and source of power than to have the Holy Spirit as our resident Divine Guest? We are told in *James 4.5* that the Holy Spirit yearns jealously for believers, to keep them from the world and close to Christ.

The Spirit moves the believer's conscience to warn of sin. He also moves their hearts when they read the Scriptures prayerfully, deepening their understanding. And at times they are so moved that they experience an unusual elevation of spirit, because the Spirit grants such a clear grasp and appreciation of what is read. As believers resist and mortify sin, the Holy Spirit strengthens them, enabling them to succeed. As they strive to pursue better attitudes, it is the Spirit who helps them to achieve love, joy, peace, and all the other elements of the fruit of the Spirit. To 'walk in the Spirit' is to have a hold on divine power, and to have the joy of certain progress in the journey of sanctification.

5. Benefit of providence

Another priceless benefit of our pilgrimage is the certainty that the Lord superintends our route, employing every situation to our eternal spiritual good, and weaving the strands of life to serve his purposes for us. *Romans 8.28* assures us – 'And we know that all things work together for good to them that love God, to them who are the called according to his purpose.' *Isaiah 41.10* declares – 'For I am with thee . . . I will help thee.'

An unbeliever may take a job in another country, and find nothing turns out as he expected, but the whole venture is a terrible mistake. He may say to himself, 'I got myself into this mess, and having made my bed I must lie in it. I have signed a contract for so many years; it will be miserable, but I only have myself to blame.' The believer's pilgrimage, however, is never quite like that, because he is able to say, 'The Lord called me to my spiritual journey and even if I stray, he will correct me, turn it to my spiritual and eternal good, and see me through.' What a difference! We are called by none other than the living God, by the Saviour of the world. When he calls, he keeps. We say, 'He will surely conduct me through to the end of the journey for I am a called person. I know that –

> *He who has led me hitherto*
> *Will lead me all my journey through.'*

'He which hath begun a good work in you will perform it until the day of Jesus Christ' *(Philippians 1.6)*. This is the work of Christ, who cannot fail. He revealed himself to us dying on Calvary for our sin, and we fell at his feet in repentance and faith, answering his call. On this journey we are not nomads or wanderers, but 'called' people, and the Lord will providentially superintend our journey.

6. Benefit of special blessings

There is yet another remarkable aspect of blessing in our pilgrim journey, expressed so vividly in *Psalm 36.7-8* – 'How excellent is thy lovingkindness, O God! therefore the children of men put their trust under the shadow of thy wings. They shall be abundantly satisfied with the fatness of thy house; and thou shalt make them drink of the river of thy pleasures.' The Christian life is not like a trek through a vast desert lacking any vestige of relief. This world certainly is a desert to believers, but there is many an oasis to refresh and lift our spirits. There is, of course, an oasis in our life every day, when we are with the Lord and his Word. And sometimes there are seasons of special happiness, tranquillity, blessing and usefulness. And then there is the rich oasis of fellowship with other members of our spiritual family, only forfeited by lofty remoteness, or a critical spirit or gossip. Then there are the countless times we stumble across an 'oasis of delight' through significant answers to prayer, fresh evidence of God's power. The Lord does not leave his people without deep encouragements, comforts and tokens of his care along the route.

Do's and don'ts of pilgrimage

We must now consider some of the do's and don'ts for pilgrims, that make such a difference to the journey. We shall address them directly to readers, the first being a serious warning: Be very careful not to settle. You are a pilgrim, don't settle! We are not talking about spiritual things here, but about earthly things. Do not put down roots and become dependent on earthly things, growing to like them too much. On the contrary, if you like something too much, don't have it, don't do it, because it will be a snare to you.

Have we not all fallen into this trap? Something very valuable has come into our life, such as a home, or an over-treasured possession, or a recreation, or clothing, and it has meant too much to us, absorbing our fascination and attention. We have become committed and dedicated to it, which is against the whole spirit of pilgrimage. Perhaps we recognised this. It was not an immoral, wrong or dreadful thing, but it engaged us too much, and by God's convicting and compelling grace we were enabled to tear it from us and to lay it aside. We reminded ourselves we were pilgrims who must be ready to move forward unimpeded, devoted to the Lord and his cause. Called to be pilgrims – passing through – we dare not settle, allowing earthly things to enfold, entrap and detain us.

Another rule for the pilgrim life is to remember that every phase of life is temporary. Are we young? Well we will not always be young. Time rolls on and we have to leave youth. The earnest pilgrim spends his youth preparing for the next phase, not clinging to the present stage. Young men have to think of marriage. In our godless age this is not seen as an obligation, but for believers it is, unless the Lord overrules. We certainly do not want anyone to develop a flirtatious spirit, but we should have a prayerful and willing heart.

In the unsaved world, when young people are asked what they aim to do in life, they generally answer by naming something they particularly enjoy, as though enjoyment is the basis of a career choice. But saved pilgrims think more of careers that will be useful and will enable them to serve the kingdom of God, and, if possible, do a good work for all people. The worldling aims at personal pleasure, gratification and fulfilment, but the pilgrim aims at service to God and good works. When young, as we have said, the pilgrim trains for the next phase of life, emulating pioneer missionaries like Hudson Taylor, who in youth restrained his diet and denied himself many reasonable comforts in order to condition and toughen himself for future service in China.

A vital *don't* for pilgrims of all ages is – never surrender spiritual priorities or waste time. I once knew a Christian man who had in his garden a beautiful and elaborate working model train system, carefully engineered and constructed over years. The engine, trucks and track were quite large, capable of carrying children, and the total impression was stunning. But how did a Christian man justify devoting so many hours, if not years, to building a gigantic toy! Let us never waste time that belongs to the Lord. One wonders what John Wesley would have done in this situation. We read that he would visit a house where silver vessels were displayed, and audaciously appropriate them for his orphanage work. Pilgrims cannot spend their time and set their hearts on earthly idols. They have a very practical approach to the material things of life.

Time, however, is not only lost in excessive attention to home, possessions and recreation, but sometimes in protracted idleness. Perhaps we have been sick or distracted by an intensive period of work or study, and unable to do all the things we would normally do for the Lord, but that period of distraction has long passed and we have never resumed our former patterns of attendance and service. Well, time is short, and we are pilgrims. We are here to make every phase of life count for the Lord, and so we must hasten back to dedicated action and weeknight attendance, resisting all the overtures of the world, the flesh and the devil. Thomas Hornblower Gill's beautiful hymn has a convicting verse:

> I would not, Lord, with swift-winged zeal
> On this world's errands go,
> And labour up the heavenly hill
> With weary feet and slow.

The hymnwriter was thinking of people who wait until later life before they wake up to serving the Lord, when all the years of energy and capability have slipped past them.

Pilgrims do not take digressions either. I once knew a man, an earnest Christian, who bought a house far bigger than he needed. It was a very beautiful detached house with umpteen bedrooms. It altogether captured his heart, but it ruined his stewardship, absorbed all his resources, and virtually consumed his life. We cannot let that kind of thing happen to us, in any area of life. We cannot take on commitments that will rule us, and negate all Christian usefulness.

Another *don't* concerns complaining and murmuring. This was the menace that drove the children of Israel round in circles, and kept them so long from their desired destination. William Cowper had the perfect cure for this expression of faithlessness:–

> *Were half the breath thus vainly spent*
> *To Heaven in supplication sent,*
> *Our cheerful song would oftener be,*
> *'Hear what the Lord has done for me.'*

Yet another *don't* is hostility between believers. Here is direct disobedience to the special law of Christ that his people should love one another. There are some professing believers who vent hostility on others, cause great hurt, and grieve away the Spirit, for years, if unchecked. We hear from pastors newly called to churches, who find there has been unresolved hostility for generations. What a tragedy! True pilgrims surely cannot allow such things to ruin their lives or their churches.

It used to be said that pilgrims are dressed for the journeying life, and so should we be. In deportment and appearance believers are clearly not worldlings who love the life of the flesh and want to take part in its lowest pursuits. True believers do not follow body-flaunting clothing styles, and message-laden 'rebel' hairstyles. The emerging churches and 'missional' churches seem to empha- sise worldly fashions, some of their middle-aged pastors absurdly presenting themselves as teenage streetwise hipsters, seemingly desperate to move as far as they can from a 'strangers and pilgrims' image.

God blesses his people with discernment and understanding if we live as pilgrims, but these faculties, like many other blessings, are conditional upon us so living. This is the message of the famous eleventh chapter of *Hebrews* – the annals of faith and pilgrimage.

The pilgrim spirit brings us rich spiritual experience, together with instrumentality and usefulness. Our own trust in God increases mightily because we prove him so much. We develop in holiness by his grace and power, and gain an ever-clearer heavenly view. We dare not linger, looking longingly at material things, or fame in this world. We should think often of the purpose and mission of the journey, and of the journey's end, and test everything with the question – 'How does this affect my pilgrimage?'

It is very sad that there is this movement among Christians, already referred to, to throw aside the pilgrim attitude. The so-called emerging and missional churches – or most of them – encourage this, proposing extraordinary things. They want believers to give up traditional church (some say give up preaching also), and be entirely informal in their worship gatherings. They think that to win worldlings to God we must be like them, going to all the films they watch (even with them), so that we can talk about them. Do the same things, they say, going with them to dances, clubs and pubs, for association is vital. Just mix, mix, mix, and live like worldlings. They don't exactly put it this way, but this is what it amounts to. We are to be more like worldlings, acting like worldlings, and matching worldlings in their activities and delights, and the more we do so, they claim, the more we will influence them.

Doctrinally liberal churches who reject the Gospel started this line of thought and action, and the missional churches have adopted it. But this policy is the exact opposite of what Bible-believing Christians have believed for centuries, and contrary to the Word of God. Nowadays one may go to any one of a number of evangelical Bible colleges in the UK and obtain a degree in 'doing church' this new way. Some of the things we hear today are so incredible, so anti-biblical, and so wrong, we are jolted when we hear them. We should never lose sight of the fact that our Saviour has called us out of the world. We should certainly be full of sympathy for lost souls, and labour for their salvation, but we will never accomplish this by rejecting the pilgrim concept of the Scriptures, and consequently grieving the Holy Spirit of God.

Says the apostle, 'I press toward the mark for the prize of the high calling of God in Christ Jesus' *(Philippians 3.14)*. We press forward as pilgrims, a people distinct from this fallen and doomed world, having been called out of it, and winning souls from it by the power of the Spirit. Our task is to call them out, not to seal them in. This is the only valid attitude to Christian living and Christian service: to live as pilgrims.

4
Sanctifying Power
And Films, Music and Leisure in the Christian Life

'That I may know him, and the power of his resurrection, and the
fellowship of his sufferings, being made conformable unto his death'
(Philippians 3.10).

THE APOSTLE writes, 'that I may know him', but he does not
mean it in quite the same sense as two verses earlier where
he counted all things loss for the excellency of the knowledge
(or the knowing) of Christ. Now he refers to knowing the power
and help of Christ in the ongoing Christian walk. This is clear from
what he proceeds to say. The subject now is striving in holiness. Paul
speaks of knowing Christ through the 'power of his resurrection'.

It is possible to misunderstand this, and think that Paul is looking forward to the future day of resurrection. Some have thought
that he desired martyrdom, and that this is what he means when
he speaks of knowing the fellowship of Christ's sufferings. But Paul
is clearly speaking about knowing resurrection power as a present

experience in his life. In other words, he refers to the continuing transformation of his own life to one of greater godliness, and he describes this process as a moral and spiritual resurrection. So, let us explore further these great words – 'that I may know him', that is, know him in sanctifying power: 'the power of his resurrection'.

Newness of life

The very same power by which Christ burst the bands of death is at work in his people in their progressive sanctification. It began to operate at conversion, when resurrection power emancipated the mind so that we grasped saving truths that previously meant nothing to us.

Perhaps you were told by a witnessing believer, 'All people are sinners,' and you would not accept it. You recoiled and said, 'That is nonsense; there are very many good people.' You could not accept that all have come short of the glory of God, and are by nature depraved, sinful and corrupt. You were appalled by the idea that no one deserved to stand before God, and that all are condemned and doomed. But then, by resurrection power, life-giving power, your eyes were opened and your view changed. You then said, 'Why could I not see this before? I see this corruption in myself. I now see it in the whole world – a world that cannot control its hatred, extortion, oppression and wars. I see sin in all commercial and private life, and I see it as I never did before in myself.' Resurrection power visited your mind, imparting a new understanding.

At the same time resurrection power transformed your character to a considerable extent, giving you a new nature, so that things that dominated you before no longer had the same power over you. You were still a sinner, but sin became your enemy, and you hated it, and longed to be free of it. New tastes, values and aspirations were planted in you, all by the life-giving power of Christ.

May the operation of that resurrection power continue to work in every believer's life, so that whenever we are confronted by time-wasting and ungodly television programmes, or any other unedifying, unproductive and even sinful attraction, the renewed will (our deciding, determining, volitional faculty) will turn our minds to better things.

Music and adventure

Let us think for a moment about our different 'leisure' pursuits and interests. What may we do in this world? There are many earthly interests, pursuits and recreations which are not directly spiritual that are permissible to believers. In a sense God has given us all things richly to enjoy. We may, for example, visit places of beauty. If we are vigorous enough we may engage in physical and sporting activities. We may like to visit places of historic interest, or engage in historical reading. Or we may have an interest in the way things work, and triumphs of human discovery, observing them and learning about them.

We may be interested and rewarded by good music and may even enjoy some degree of illuminating fiction, but for all such things we have to be sure they are wholesome. We would not bar the young from exposure to adventure, and even the spectacular. There are many things which can legitimately appeal to our minds and occupy and engage us. But whatever we do, we have to keep godly standards, and apply tests. Also, we must ration even legitimate things, otherwise they will replace Christ and his service, and hinder the spiritual resurrection process going on in our lives, ruining our tastes.

Modern entertainment music of the worst kind is everywhere, intruding into life constantly. In the past Christians ignored popular songs, regarding them as part of this world and belonging to the old life. Around the mid-1950s pop songs took a steep dive, becoming even worse in moral content than they were before, constituting an obvious, orchestrated campaign against God's standards, and promoting the very opposite conduct. The world of popular entertainment music increasingly became an all-out assault against authority, order and refinement, contending for unrestrained sexual indulgence, self-love and self-gratification.

This culture became a powerful and dangerous message, opposed to everything holy and noble. Amazingly, as it unfolded, many Christian people broke with their tradition of standing aloof, and capitulated to its alluring rhythms and lyrics. But it was a 'propaganda' culture designed to bring society away from God and into rebellion against him. Christians have no business accommodating what their forebears rejected.

To adapt and adopt the music of the entertainment world for worship was an astonishing development, and certainly disobedient to the overwhelming commands and principles of Scripture. It is wrong to employ it in worship, and equally wrong to embrace it in personal leisure and pleasure. People have said to me that they listen to rock and pop, even as believers. Some have acknowledged that they had a conscience about it when they were first converted, but they subsequently overrode that, and pushed those thoughts away.

Dear friends, this is of the world. This is the production of the prince of the power of the air, channelled to society from drug-influenced groups of notoriously ungodly and rebellious entertainers. It was created to capture people. Delivered in powerful rhythmic form, it is emotional manipulation, euphoric and designed to enslave. If we have succumbed to this in our church or home lives, it is vital that we come before the Lord in deep regret and repentance, and begin to practise discernment, and repudiate it. It is against all principles and order, not to mention reverence, and it will certainly eclipse the privilege of knowing resurrection power in our lives.

I remember reading some years ago an article by a professing Christian young man who had begun to indulge deeply in entertainment music. When he went to church he began to find everything extremely dull and drab. It ceased to be to his taste. He told of how hymns became empty and boring, and nothing could uplift him.

Obviously, what ruled his private life had changed him and wrecked his spiritual sensitivities and tastes. His spirit now looked for entertainment, for the emotional impact provided by an audio-drug, and not for the blessings of Truth. In the event this man became the founder of a group of charismatic rock-music churches. The secular entertainment music captured his soul.

There are doubtless many things we can employ and enjoy in this present world. But there are also things deeply stained by today's depraved standards, such as the world of films. There is not much that believers should want to see. We need always to ask – Is it clean? Is it pure? Is it wholesome? Is it edifying? Could I take the Lord there? Could I have him next to me?

We need to ask the questions, judge and weigh the matter conscientiously, or we disrupt the 'moral resurrection' process in our lives, and dishonour the Lord. Only if something is clean and wholesome should we watch it or listen to it, and even then, we should ration our indulgence. Christian magazines and blogs that review and approve entertainment films and videos show their contempt for an authentic Christian life and the pursuit of holiness. We may be able to watch some of what is on television, but the standards just mentioned must always apply.

This brings us to the question – Do we turn on the television on the Lord's Day, other, say, than for a news bulletin? Surely we should never do so! It is the Lord's Day, dear Christian friends! This is the day designated for him, and for his worship and service. Consider Paul's words – 'That I may know him'. They apply supremely to the Lord's Day, our day of dedication, reflection and fellowship, and our day to make him known. We cannot 'know him' and allow entertainment media to take over our lives at the same time.

Our verse says – 'That I may know him, and the power of his resurrection, and the fellowship of his sufferings'. What does it mean to know the fellowship of his sufferings? Equally, what does it mean to be 'made conformable unto his death'?

We have noted that some teachers think Paul had an ambition to be martyred for Christ, but that is probably not the meaning here. The subject is still knowing resurrection power to change and shape us. We remember that our Saviour suffered and died on Calvary to purchase our everlasting salvation, but also so that we should live holy lives in this life. To have fellowship in his sufferings means I live so as to make his sufferings worthwhile and effective in my life. They will, of course, be effective to purchase my eternal soul, but are they motivating me to strive for righteousness in my earthly life?

Let me illustrate it in this way. A student must now pay top-up fees to go to university. Supposing someone scrimped and saved to enable you to go to university, and gave you the money, but you gambled it away. Astonishing! Someone made a great sacrifice, and you gambled it away! Christ has suffered not only to secure our salvation, but also to bring us on to the road of striving after holiness. Do we squander the blessing and neglect the process of moral resurrection? To be a partaker of his sufferings means we live to honour them.

To slightly change the illustration, someone buys us a home, not merely giving a deposit, but the total sum, and we gamble it away. Unthinkable! This is a poor illustration, but it is as though Christ suffered and died to make me righteous, and I fritter away the benefit. I do not even try to live a righteous life, separate from the tainted and corrupt culture of this world. I turn on the television and watch anything, including scandalous things, even on the Lord's Day. Christ suffered and died not only to purchase my salvation, but to deliver me from ongoing participation in smut, filth, material idolatry, and all other things that are offensive to him.

Perhaps someone is watching films that are utterly unsuitable for a believer, and which taint him and bring him down. Also all day long he allows the world to ram beat music into his head. He comes to depend on it to lift his mood. It really dominates and rules him. It seems he cannot live without it. Such a believer is not walking in fellowship with his Lord's sufferings. He is not conforming to their purpose. Christ died to make me an altogether better person, and so I will strive by his help to resist sin. That is fellowship with his sufferings. He made the sacrifice so that I could live the life. What he died for, I will live for. That is 'being made conformable unto his death'. The apostle uses this same kind of argument throughout *Romans 6*, relating our Saviour's death and resurrection to our present sanctification.

Philippians 3.11 and following confirm that Paul is speaking of the present work of sanctification in our lives, and the striving and effort involved. 'If by any means,' he says, 'I might attain unto the resurrection of the dead'. It is obvious that he is not referring to his future resurrection, for he would never speak about that as if it were uncertain. He would say – 'I know I shall attain unto the resurrection of the dead.' He would confidently assert that Christ will never leave him nor forsake him.

But in this eleventh verse he is speaking of the believer's present, progressive, moral resurrection, which we may frustrate and hinder. The language is therefore less certain: 'If by any means I might attain unto the resurrection of the dead'. Surely we should say, in the same way, 'If only in the days of this coming week I might exercise more caution, more judgement, and weigh more carefully the things I do. If only I might reject the sinful, unprofitable things that would steal my spiritual tastes, waste my time and corrupt me.'

'Not as though I had already attained', Paul proceeds to say, further confirming that he has been speaking about our present moral resurrection. We notice that this is a progressive work. He has not fully attained, nor is he complete, but, he says, 'I follow after.' Paul seems to say, with great fervour, 'My Lord has died for me, and grasped hold of me with arms of love. He has changed me and made me his own, and I long to grasp him, to be nearer to him, to know him better, and be more conformed to his holy standards. So I pursue, I press after him.'

We cannot fail to see the language of effort, concern, diligence, and conscientious Christian living. Is this true of us? So important is this 'pursuit' that Paul repeats himself (verses 13-14) – 'Brethren, I count not myself to have apprehended *[grasped]*: but this one thing I do, forgetting those things which are behind *[the old life, with its sinful delights and distractions and unprofitable things]*, and reaching forth unto those things which are before, I press toward the mark for the prize of the high calling of God in Christ Jesus.'

What are we like? Are we casual in our spiritual lives? Do we just dream through the days, or do we strain and stretch? Do we weigh things, asking – Is this moral? Is this for Christ? Or is this promoting the world? Is this intoxicating? (We remember Paul's words, 'I will not be brought under the power of any.') Am I living carelessly or carefully? Let us say – I determine to be conscientious, to honour my Lord. I desire the resurrection process in my life. I want to know more of his power. I long for more prayer, and more instrumentality in a ministry of intercession.

Many things are permissible to us, and we should take an interest in earthly things, but we need strength of mind to ceaselessly assess and weigh them, and strength to ration the things we engage in. We have the help of Christ. We have all his mighty power. Think of the power he exercised at the resurrection when his soul was united with his body, and he broke the bands of death, re-infusing life into his own body, and rising from the dead. That power is available to us from the living Christ to renew our minds, our wills, our tastes, our desires, every part of us. It is that for which we must long and pray.

5
Aspirations of Christian Service

'For we are labourers together with God' *(1 Corinthians 3.9)*.

THE RANGE OF TERMS used in the New Testament to describe those who represent the mission of Christ presents a great challenge and standard for all who love the Lord. Whether the office of *apostle* or the role of a *herald*, or whether the work of *ambassador* or *farmer* or *master builder*, the terms teem with objectives for us all. And who cannot be challenged by the spiritually equivalent functions of *athlete, soldier, steward* and even *slave*? All these terms jolt us from complacency, and display the qualities we should press for in our service for Christ. And a desire to serve the Lord is a mark of Christian character.

You might say that this is a theme for pastors, evangelists, elders and deacons, but in a priesthood of all believers all share these tasks to a large degree, and all should know the functions and effort intended by each term. On the one hand, how can pastors and other office bearers be held accountable if the members have only a shallow idea of their intended duties and qualities, and on the other, how can the members know their own true calling without understanding these Christian service metaphors?

1. The apostle

The first term to be considered is that of *apostle*, meaning a messenger, literally one who is sent. In the New Testament it describes those who had a special office, namely the twelve that were appointed by the Lord, including the replacement for Judas, and of course the apostle Paul, the 'one born out of due time'. These men were more than just messengers, having special and unique authority. However, the term is also very occasionally used to describe an ordinary evangelist or church planter. Barnabas is called an apostle (in this lesser sense) and so are Silas and Timothy. They were men sent to the unconverted, sent from the church to the world, prototypes of all preachers and Christian workers who are called to proclaim as widely as possible the message of God. This use of the term *apostle* focuses our attention on outsiders, on lost souls.

Strangely, at the present time many evangelical preachers do not practise the preaching of specifically evangelistic, persuasive sermons, but just 'put in a word' for the unsaved here and there in sermons designed for the edifying of believers. Some other preachers, who do believe in dedicated evangelistic sermons, only preach them occasionally. Either position is an enormous tragedy, because the ethos of the New Testament mission church is thereby lost, and blessing forfeited. The term *apostle* surely reminds us we are *sent* to a lost world, and this must be uppermost in our minds in our proclamation of the Word.

Sometimes people protest that the task of reaching the unsaved cannot be done by preaching within the walls of a church, and they are partly right. It is obviously essential to reach out in witness and visitation, but proclaiming the Gospel in a building became central to witness from the earliest days of the young church. At first, evangelistic preaching took place in the open air, but wherever possible, it also moved into buildings. At Ephesus, for example, Paul took the bulk of his preaching into 'the school of one Tyrannus', so the preaching came indoors, believers no doubt bringing people in. Indoors, the preaching could be carried out more freely without interruption.

In *1 Corinthians 14.23-24* we are given a picture of such a public meeting. Before the withdrawal by God of the gift of tongues, some disorderly exercise of that gift took place in the Corinthian church, and the apostle warned that if people came in from the outside they would think Christians were mad. We note that outsiders were coming in to hear the Word. *James 2* also gives an insight into public meetings visited by unsaved people. James warns churches not to take the rich person to the best seat while directing the poor to sit on the floor.

It is interesting to observe how great revivals beginning in the open air very soon moved into buildings. In south London in 1739, the Kennington Common (along with other places) saw tremendous crowds listening to George Whitefield, but very soon buildings were erected, where the preachers were safe from hurled bricks and clamour. A huge Tabernacle was constructed for Whitefield in central London, and the same happened for the Wesley brothers. But whether working in open fields or church buildings, the original calling of the preacher was that he should be primarily an 'apostle', one *sent* from God to a lost world. Is this the first priority of pastors today, and of all other believers also?

2. The herald

A second significant term to note is that of *herald*. Almost every time we see the words *preach* or *preacher* in the New Testament, the Greek signifies a herald. 'I am ordained a preacher,' says the apostle *(1 Timothy 2.7)*. The secular herald was often a town crier who gave vital news and information to the public from the town elders. All civic instructions, commands, edicts and news, went to such a herald, who would stand in prominent places and let his voice reach as many people as possible. The significance of the term *herald* is parallel with that of *apostle.*

Nowadays people often complain that information about road closures and other such matters are announced in barely-read local newspapers, but in former times the herald's job was to inform as many citizens as he could. The term provides a compelling illustration of the commission given to Christian preachers, and to the church membership as a whole. Certainly preachers should declare all the truth of the Word, but without losing sight of the fact that they are commissioned to bring as many people as possible under the saving Word. As we have noted, numerous Bible-believing churches have virtually no Gospel proclamation at all. Heralding the Gospel is our foremost task.

3. The ambassador

In *2 Corinthians 5.20* we find another term – 'Now then we are *ambassadors* for Christ, as though God did beseech you by us: we pray you in Christ's stead, be ye reconciled to God.' *Ambassador* in the Greek literally means a senior, an elder, a presbyter, but here it indicates a representative of the king in a foreign land. In *Ephesians 6*, Paul describes himself as 'an ambassador in bonds'. Even when in prison, the greatest burden on his mind was to be addressing whoever he could, reaching out for souls, and the Lord gave him unexpected opportunities, even preaching before kings and procurators while under arrest.

An ambassador knows the king's policy and represents it to a foreign sovereign, stating his king's views precisely. He does not invent his message or adapt it. He has no power or authority to create a policy for his king, but only to present his instructions exactly. He does his work courteously, and yet persuasively. He may often be resented, even reviled, but he must remain faithful. The experts tell us that an ambassador in ancient times would always represent his home culture. The application for us is that we should not adopt *worldly* culture, or live like worldlings. We are in a foreign land representing God's holiness and mercy, and we have a holy office to discharge.

Believers are not concerned only with their own church community, but are ambassadors of salvation and Christian values to a lost world, and they are accountable to God for the extent to which this is accomplished. *Ambassador* is a strong and guiding term, rebuking the present-day drift of churches into innovations and conformity with the world, and calling us to the faithful proclamation of the saving Word that God has provided.

4. The steward

A striking term is found in *1 Corinthians 4.1* – 'Let a man so account of us, as of the ministers of Christ, and *stewards* of the mysteries of God.' A steward had considerable responsibility on his shoulders in biblical days. He was the manager of an estate, responsible for buying and selling, the payment of wages, and the custodian and distributor of his master's charitable bounty. The term appears (though translated differently) in *1 Corinthians 9.16-17* where Paul is speaking about preaching the Gospel:–

> 'For though I preach the gospel, I have nothing to glory of: for necessity is laid upon me; yea, woe is unto me, if I preach not the gospel! For if I do this thing willingly, I have a reward: but if against my will, a dispensation *[literally a stewardship, a distributorship]* of the gospel is committed unto me.'

Elsewhere Paul calls preachers *stewards* of the mysteries of grace. A steward, being a treasurer, had to be reliable, for he settled the bills, and hired the staff and day labourers. He arranged also all repairs, and paid out for grain and seed. As we have mentioned, he dispensed compassionate help, large landholders often providing for the poor and dispossessed. It is this aspect of the steward's work that is chiefly in mind when the 'steward' term is applied to Gospel work. An unreliable steward might neglect to distribute alms, or even pocket them. The preacher is accountable to God for the distribution of the Gospel to as many people as need it. He must frequently ask himself what he will have to say for himself when called to give account of his stewardship, but every believer must feel accountable also. What have we done with the tremendous bounty, the treasure of the Gospel, for which we have been made responsible? This is our supreme task, to be stewards or distributors of God's saving riches.

5. The farmer

The next term to note is that of *farmer*, suggested in *1 Corinthians 3.6-9* where Paul says – 'I have planted, Apollos watered; but God gave the increase…' *2 Timothy 2.6* employs the same illustration, Paul casting us as farmers or husbandmen. We are to do the planting and pruning work, but of course it is the Spirit of God whose power is responsible for everything that is accomplished. What an apt illustration this is, because a farmer depends upon the climate, the soil, and forces outside his control, to produce the crop, just as we depend upon the Spirit, but he must still labour.

Some take a highly romantic attitude to Gospel work, thinking all you have to do is pray to God for revival, and he will do everything for you, but Paul says we are farmers, and although we acknowledge that only God can give the increase, yet we must prepare and plough. It is hard and protracted work, and cannot be disregarded. Thorns must be uprooted, then sowing and ultimately reaping carried out. Before high mechanisation, these were humbling, hard, labouring tasks. They were also constant tasks. The farmer could not take a year off, or leave out a vital stage, such as the sowing of the grain, and in our Gospel ministry we too can leave no stage out. We have to cover every aspect of the work of reaching people.

Further, this is a patient task which cannot be hurried. There is a time to sow and there is a time to reap; the calendar cannot be altered, nor compressed. We have seen the fad of mass evangelism, where people have chosen to concentrate on 'crash' evangelism at long intervals. The idea has been to get thousands of people together in a stadium venue, lay on an impressive choir and other attractions (these days including contemporary music groups), and use a dynamic communicator to lean on the emotions of the crowd. The aim is to engineer the saving of many in a few weeks of a crusade. How much more convenient that seems than to engage in constant visitation and Gospel preaching in the local church. But evangelism cannot be forced into a mould to suit our convenience, and time has shown that modern organised mass evangelism falls far, far short of its boasted claims. In reality, it has usually brought into our churches short-lived and inauthentic 'fruits'.

The overriding objective in farming is to bring in a certain and bountiful crop, an increase, by steady toil. The pastor, the preacher, must not focus entirely on feeding the flock and expounding the Scripture, for the farming term shows he is also engaged, with the whole church, in a crop-bearing activity.

6. The master builder

A similarly remarkable term for Christian service appears in *1 Corinthians 3.10* – that of a wise *master builder*. The Greek indicates an architect, but of course the Christian communicator does not invent or design the Gospel, 'for other foundation can no man lay than that is laid, which is Jesus Christ.' Nevertheless, a congregation must be won and built up wisely in accordance with God's message and principles.

Paul describes the differing types of construction. On the one hand, one may 'build upon this foundation gold, silver, precious stones', meaning, real converts who have been convicted of sin, and have truly repented and come to the Lord. On the other hand, one may build 'wood, hay, stubble' – referring to false converts who have been rushed into a decision and have come to Christ without genuine repentance, faith, and surrender of their old lives. In this latter case, the congregation will not be a genuine church, but at best a mixture, and perhaps entirely composed of wood, hay and stubble. 'Every man's work,' Paul continues, 'shall be made manifest: for the day shall declare it, because it shall be revealed by fire.' It will be seen in the last day that many churches consist of 'converts' that are the fruit of a shallow message by which people have not been eternally saved.

The apostle's analysis contains a shocking and challenging fact, for we discover that a preacher who has built the false church may actually be a genuine believer. 'If any man's work abide which he hath built thereupon, he shall receive a reward.' However – 'If any man's work shall be burned, he shall suffer loss: but he himself shall be saved; yet so as by fire.' The foolish builder will be saved, even though the church he has built will be burned up. There could be no more powerful warning to be always concerned to proclaim the Gospel of repentance, and to pray that people will undergo real conversion. They must not be rushed through the gates of baptism and church membership too quickly.

There is much to learn from the illustration of the builder. The plan of God must be followed and the right order maintained, beginning with the foundation and building upwards. All witness and evangelism starts with repentance. When churches are filled with false converts, cracks soon appear, and decadent trends pour in. Worldly entertainment-style music, worldly dress and behaviour are enthusiastically adopted and the historic distinction between church and world is thrown down. Preachers and office bearers first are to be wise master builders, and all the members must stand with them and behind them in this duty of discernment and care. It is a hallmark of Christian character.

7. The athlete

A very different term for the work of Christian workers is identified by *1 Corinthians 9.24.* 'Know ye not that they which run in a race run all, but one receiveth the prize?' Christ's servants are to be *athletes* in a spiritual sense. Like athletes they should be committed to making the maximum effort constantly. Earthly appetites must be restrained, and all endeavours prepared for. 'Now they do it,' says Paul, 'to obtain a corruptible crown; but we an incorruptible. I therefore so run, not as uncertainly; so fight I *[the illustration changes to a boxer or wrestler]*, not as one that beateth the air: but I keep under my body, and bring it into subjection: lest that by any means, when I have preached to others, I myself should be a castaway.' (The word *castaway* does not mean spiritually lost, but rejected by God for service, because the work was not accompanied by holy living.)

Paul speaks of striving 'for mastery' in the proclamation of the Gospel. The context is the preaching of the Gospel (verses 16-23) and while holiness is certainly in view, it is the work of soul winning that gives rise to the 'athlete' analogy. The life of Christian service involves tremendous application and effort. An opponent is in view, a runner, or a wrestler even. Earthly athletes will only have to strive and struggle while young, and very soon, perhaps by mid-to-late twenties, will no longer be competitive, and will cease training and take their ease. The servant of God, however, the proclaimer for Christ, will be a lifelong athlete. His opponent is the devil, who will be determined to prevent or obstruct his service. He must remain determined, and grieved at losing or falling behind.

The athlete accepts sacrifice and pain, striving for constant improvement. Do we, in the Lord's service? In preaching, in teaching, in Sunday School work, or in personal witness, do we often say, 'I could have done that better'? We should constantly review and assess. Secular businesses follow a policy of constant improvement, but we are seeking a far more important goal, the rescue of souls.

We believe that the work is the Lord's, and it is only by the Spirit that people are saved, but also we believe that God employs human instruments, and so we must be wholly and zealously engaged, with the intense dedication of athletes.

8. The slave

One of the most frequently used terms for Christian workers appears at first glance to be the least noble, namely that of a *slave*. Paul describes himself as 'a servant of Jesus Christ, called to be an apostle'. Wherever we see the word *servant* used by the apostle, it is a translation of the word *slave*. He calls himself a slave of Christ, and every Christian worker is a willing bondslave of the Lord. This is how we are to see ourselves. As his slaves we are never off duty, and we claim no rights.

Until quite recently, because of the spiritual nature of his duties, a minister was generally not regarded by the law as an employee of his church. This meant that he had no right to go to an employment tribunal to complain about his treatment by the church, and a trade union that represented some ministers campaigned for a change in this law. Paul, however, is glad to be a bondslave of Christ with no rights, glad to follow the commands of the Lord, and this should be the attitude of all of us.

Wherever the Lord posts us, we will go. Whatever he calls us to do, we will carry it out. We will covet no time-consuming hobbies, but will be entirely for him. We are the property of Christ (and his church), gladly surrendering self-indulgence and personal aims in this world. We are subject to his calling and direction.

If we are preachers we will claim no right to be selective in our tasks, saying, for example, 'I am called to be an expositor, not an evangelist.' Christ has called us to learn to be everything, and we will assert no right to pick and choose. 'Slave' is probably Paul's favourite term to describe himself and other servants of Christ in the glorious work of the Gospel, and this term is the calling of every believer in

Christ. Am I – we should ask ourselves – really a willing slave of the Lord who bought me?

9. The soldier

Our ninth and final term describing the Christian worker is in *2 Timothy 2.3-4*. 'Thou therefore endure hardness, as a good *soldier* of Jesus Christ. No man that warreth entangleth himself with the affairs of this life; that he may please him who hath chosen him to be a soldier.' A combatant soldier, when he came to the battlefield – the place of blood and agony and death – trembled with anxiety. And we who are on the spiritual battlefield cannot approach it in a spirit of flippancy. This is the most serious work in the world.

A soldier accepts danger, knowing he could die for the cause at any time, and he accepts that. How much more should Christians accept inconvenience or setbacks. A soldier in the field accepts rations, uniform and injury, and so does the Christian worker. His means will often be limited, his work defined for him, insults, hurts and hindrances assail, but all must be sustained with good grace and faithful prayer. Victory is essential to the earthly soldier, not optional. He does not go into battle merely hoping that something perhaps might be gained, but knows he must succeed or be humiliated, and he exerts himself accordingly. Our calling is to proclaim and defend the faith, and to win souls.

In days of ease and plenty, churches die for want of the spirit of military conflict – the noble war for souls and Truth. Often even the minsters, the preachers, are at ease, leaving little hope for dwindling congregations.

* * *

All who feel that God is leading them to preach the Gospel should reflect on all these terms, praying that God will inspire their hearts with the aims, objectives, and attitudes they entail. Yet the terms should be reflected in all believers, for we are all commissioned to reach lost souls, all being in some measure 'sent ones' or *apostles*.

As *heralds* we are to attempt to take the message of mercy to a rebellious world. As *ambassadors* we represent the King of Heaven, and must maintain our distinctiveness and separation from the godless culture around us. As *stewards* we are accountable for how we distribute Gospel riches. As *farmers* we must on no account neglect the laborious work of ploughing and sowing, along with every other agricultural process until we reap the crop. As *builders* we must conscientiously follow God's master plan (so often ignored by the innovations and gimmicks of today), constructing upon the foundation of Christ. As *athletes* we strive with all the effort, preparation and sacrifice necessary. As *bondslaves* we are to renounce self-consideration, and consider no burden too much to win the greatest accolade, 'Well done, thou good and faithful *servant.*' As *soldiers* we are to serve as those who see the saving of souls as a life or death conflict.

If these are our aspirations then the Lord, who placed all these great terms in his Word, will mightily help us, and be with us.

6
Christian Mutual Helpfulness
The Seven Aims of Personal Ministry

'And I myself also am persuaded of you, my brethren, that ye also are full of goodness, filled with all knowledge, able also to admonish one another' *(Romans 15.14)*.

OVER THE LAST 40 YEARS, there has come in among Christians a great craze for counselling borrowed from the ideas of secular psychology, largely formulated by militant atheists holding a view of human personality and morality altogether opposed to biblical teaching. It is astonishing that evangelical seminaries have enthusiastically adopted their systems, larger churches hiring teams of counsellors to 'heal' Christians – who need biblical ministry and counsel, not psychological therapy. The so-called biblical counselling movement has abandoned the doctrine of the absolute sufficiency of the Bible for guidance and sanctification of believers, but we must cling to the inspired Word alone, and keep to traditional scriptural methodology when advising on personal problems, whether of depression or of behaviour.

Of course, we acknowledge that when it comes to very serious and painful depression, or irrational and delusional behaviour, the problem lies outside the troubles of 'normal' life. The afflicted person is ill and in need of medical help. The disaster of the 'counselling movement', however, is that it treats all believers as if they were psychologically ill, which is humanistic foolishness. In a company of a hundred Christians, there may typically be three or four people who will suffer the level of depression or other mental illness that requires medical help. If someone is really sick in mind, or has a breakdown of such a kind that they lose touch with reality, or are likely to do themselves or others considerable harm, then, sadly, they are ill, and need appropriate help.

We are not talking about such needs here. When we mention 'depression' we have in mind the kind which most people have at some time, perhaps involving sorrow, regret, distress, worry, anxiety, frustration, the sense of unfittedness, and even a measure of panic, all of which are within the 'normal' experience of life. In the past the trials of life were never placed into the category of illness, requiring psychological therapy, and Christians believed that the Lord had given the riches of the Word to enable his people to draw close to him, and to be strengthened and comforted.

What does today's 'Christian' counselling do? As Dr Martin Bobgan points out in several books analysing the techniques of 'Christian' pseudo-psychology, it attempts to deal with problems rather than with people. The Bible is exactly the other way round. If we have a marriage difficulty, the Bible does not tell us to complete a questionnaire detailing all our tastes and tiffs, and then find a counsellor to work through each problem. The Bible directly addresses our character, reforming us, making us more holy, and showing us how to live by the power of the Spirit, so that we manifest kindness and understanding, putting the other person first, and being better people. According to the Bible, if we become holy, then the marital problems will be overcome. While counselling books deal endlessly with the symptoms, the Bible reforms the person.

The Christian counselling movement is now a vast industry, and the number of books produced is phenomenal. As believers, we should reject virtually all of these, even though many of the authors are evangelical, because they have capitulated to the anti-biblical ideas of atheistic psychology.

We now turn to the positive side of how all Christians should participate, as need arises, in the ministry of mutual admonition or mutual personal helpfulness, beginning with a very brief review of the texts that urge us to do this. Subsequently we shall look at biblical exhortations about the right attitude and approach, and then consider the seven great objectives or aims of this precious ministry.

The duty of mutual admonition

Our *Romans 15.14* text presents the duty and the rules of true personal ministry among believers, Paul writing: 'I myself also am persuaded of you, my brethren, that ye also are full of goodness, filled with all knowledge, able also to admonish one another.' The Greek word for 'admonish' means 'to place in the mind'. It may be an exhortation, or a warning in the form of a warm, friendly urging to honour some duty or objective. We often connect admonition with words of reproof, but the Greek term has a broader use than that. What is placed in the mind may certainly be a caution or reproof, but it may equally be the gentlest suggestion or words of encouragement. Three other verses on the place of admonition should also influence us, the first being *Colossians 3.16*:

> 'Let the word of Christ dwell in you richly in all wisdom; teaching and admonishing one another in psalms and hymns and spiritual songs, singing with grace in your hearts to the Lord.'

Noted exegetes say that the semi-colon in this verse rightly belongs after the words 'one another', for we admonish by the Word. So, for example, if we see some friend who is not attending meetings regularly, or if we see another sliding into covetousness, then prayerfully we get alongside to bring the standards of the Word, for we all have a part in the ministry of admonishing one another.

We should also respond to the letter to the *Hebrews 3.12-13*:

> 'Take heed, brethren, lest there be in any of you an evil heart of unbelief, in departing from the living God. But exhort one another daily, while it is called to day; lest any of you be hardened through the deceitfulness of sin.'

Here is the duty of believers to help each other check any decline, and to intervene and assist wherever necessary and wherever possible. Of course, we have to cultivate the right spirit, and we will touch on that in a moment, but first we quote from *Hebrews 10.23-24*:

> 'Let us hold fast the profession of our faith without wavering; (for he is faithful that promised;) and let us consider one another to provoke unto love and to good works.'

The admonition term is not specifically used here, but it is the same thought. We have a duty of mutual helpfulness. Returning to *Romans 15.14*, we are given some of the qualifications for this ministry, Paul saying that the people were full of goodness, and filled with all knowledge. Goodness (meaning the qualities of kindness and consideration) is essential if we are to counsel others. Equally it is vital to be 'filled with all knowledge', which refers to knowledge of the Bible, not of human wisdom. Make no mistake, this is a dangerous ministry, with the potential, if mishandled, to injure friendships, and even whole fellowships. For this reason anyone who admonishes another must take time in self-examination, considering some of the qualifications required, and the spirit in which this ministry must be exercised. Here are some biblical counsels for mutual admonition.

The first counsel is found in *Luke 6.37* and *41*:

> 'Judge not, and ye shall not be judged: condemn not, and ye shall not be condemned: forgive, and ye shall be forgiven ... And why beholdest thou the mote that is in thy brother's eye, but perceivest not the beam that is in thine own eye?'

This caution highlights the disaster of a superior or critical spirit in helping one another. Admonition must be approached with humility, considering (or examining) ourselves, 'lest thou also be tempted' *(Galatians 6.1)*. We all have many sins, failings, weaknesses and difficulties, of which we should be deeply aware. We will ourselves fall in some respect, and need the help and even the reproof of others, and we are to approach one another in that humble spirit of awareness. Our humility or lack of it is very apparent to the person we seek to help, and makes our admonition acceptable or odious. Certainly the person who hands out advice from a dizzy height is never acceptable.

A second counsel from the words of the Lord calls us to be ready to share our own spiritual lessons and experiences. *Luke 6.45* reads:

> 'A good man out of the good treasure of his heart bringeth forth that which is good; and an evil man...that which is evil.'

The treasure refers to gracious deeds and also to edifying conversation, and when applied to the ministry of admonition, the 'good man' naturally urges and comforts from the wealth of his experience of God's grace toward him. Giving admonition can be a very humbling experience. If we see someone heading into a problem that we ourselves once had, we must be ready to acknowledge that we did that same foolish thing and fell into a snare. 'I am afraid,' we may say, 'that you are doing the same.' Admonition, as we have noted, is not from a dizzy height. Our counsel will come from the Bible, and will often be supplemented from our own experience of failure and recovery, and we must be ready for this.

In *Luke 17.1-2* (our third counsel) there is an unusually solemn and serious caution, and while the verse primarily applies to the young, it obviously applies more widely also to all God's children.

> 'It is impossible but that offences will come: but woe unto him, through whom they come! It were better for him that a millstone were hanged about his neck, and he cast into the sea, than that he should offend one of these little ones.'

This third counsel for the ministry of personal admonition is that there should be no callous, rough, attacking interrogation, and no hasty presumption of guilt. It is amazing what one hears about the conduct of some Christians, even pastors, about their approach to admonition. We have to be scrupulously careful, fair and well moderated in this ministry, and not leap to conclusions and judgements. For one thing, the problem we think we see in that person may not be the true picture, and we may have misread the apparent evidence. The person may be entirely innocent, or there may be factors which greatly reduce any blame. Further, the 'straying' person may have been admonished by others already, and will feel caught in an avalanche of condemnation. Admonition never sets out to inflict pain, dislike, irritation or vengeance, and if it does, according to Christ's caution, the admonisher becomes the guilty party. So we deal with one another as respected and valued fellow-believers, and never in a rough, cavalier kind of way.

Our fourth counsel is from *Luke 17.3-4*:

'Take heed to yourselves: If thy brother trespass against thee, rebuke him; and if he repent, forgive him. And if he trespass against thee seven times in a day, and seven times in a day turn again to thee, saying, I repent; thou shalt forgive him.'

The key point here is that motive matters. To be qualified to engage in mutual shepherding we must possess a sincere desire to see advance, rather than to masquerade as a senior believer, or a reformer or corrector of others for personal gratification. What is our motive? Is it really to help, and to see the Lord glorified and his work speeded forward? Is there true sympathy in our heart? In *Romans 12.15*, Paul writes, 'Rejoice with them that do rejoice, and weep with them that weep.' There is a still higher outcome to be gained than the reformation of the erring brother or sister. This is the spirit of mutual personal ministry.

A fifth counsel for admonition is drawn from *Romans 15.14* and *Colossians 3.16*: 'teaching and admonishing *one another*'. The question for us is: Are we ourselves willing to be admonished, warned, urged, or helped by others? If we are not, we are certainly not qualified or in a fit condition to admonish. If we are touchy, prickly, proud or sensitive when someone says to us: 'You should not have done that,' then we should not try giving admonition ourselves. Personal ministry is two-way traffic, and a lack of humility to receive it is quickly detected. The one we seek to help or correct can see perfectly well that we are not the kind of person who would take kindly to returned admonition.

The sixth counsel is this – a bond is the best basis for admonition. In *Colossians 3.14* we read:

> 'And above all these things put on charity, which is the bond of perfectness.'

These words occur just two verses before the exhortation to engage in mutual admonition, and there is obviously a connection. Do we have a bond with the person whom we intend to admonish? Is there a basis of friendship and respect, or is the person relatively unknown to us, in which case it would be better to let another, better-placed, person do the work. Love covers a multitude of sins in various ways, and wayward believers, or those in need of advice, will receive it most readily from someone who knows and values them.

The seventh counsel comes from *1 Peter 5.2-3*, and it is another qualification, namely – Have we set an example? Peter's words are primarily to ministers, but they apply to all engaging in an act of mutual admonition:

> 'Feed the flock of God which is among you, taking the oversight thereof, not by constraint, but willingly; not for filthy lucre, but of a ready mind; neither as being lords over God's heritage, but being ensamples [patterns] to the flock.'

Have we set an example before we speak? If our own walk is inconsistent, and we manifest conspicuous, unaddressed faults, we obviously cannot help others. To extend this point, in *1 Timothy 4.16* we read: 'Take heed unto thyself, and unto the doctrine;

continue in them.' Only those who are conscientiously concerned for personal sanctification should venture to assist others in their walk. Do we strive for right conduct in our inner life, and in our family and church life? Are we those who hunger and thirst after it?

* * *

Following these cautions we come to seven great aims of personal ministry. If readers are familiar with the new genre of counselling books, chiefly drawn from secular 'insights', they will notice at once that the aims set out here are about changing people, rather than only their behaviour. The advice offered here is not novel but very old, the kind of aims and objectives that believers would have been given in Reformation times, in Puritan times, and in Victorian times, in fact, right up until the 1970s when secular psychology suddenly became more attractive to many in the evangelical realm than the Bible.

THE SEVEN AIMS
1. Holiness is the goal

The most obvious aim of mutual admonition is that of assisting holiness and character. Our *Romans 15.14* text makes 'full of goodness' the qualification for mutual admonition, and it is also the main aim. Take marriage problems, referred to earlier. Should we convene a number of 'counselling' sessions, giving time for 'digging and delving', setting of homework and assignments, and all the other elaborations of the counselling books? Or should we be encouraging personal godliness, so that our hearers advance as people? All the rules for marriage are set out in the magnificent thirteenth chapter of *1 Corinthians*, and also in *Ephesians 4* and *5*. They are the great aspirations for Christian relationships, and if only we can explain and commend these to those in trouble, their marriages would repair and blossom gloriously.

Take *1 Peter 3.7*, where we learn that a spouse should be held in honour, meaning in esteem, with dignity, care and love. In effect, husbands and wives must be precious to one another, each showing appreciation, kindness and consideration, all of which flow from godly character. If only they can build up godly character by the help of God, they will become much nicer people, and their marriage will be honouring to the Lord. Each will be considerate, and will give and do for the other everything they ought to. It is the person or people that the Lord changes, so that problems are resolved. A good book on marriage will be one that simply expounds these passages.

The characteristics of love in *1 Corinthians 13* are the best and the most profound statements on the subject in all literature, and this is so because they are of divine origin. The first aim of personal ministry is to urge one another to character and godliness, and not to intrude into the nuts and bolts of private behaviour, which, in the case of marriage, also betrays and fractures the bond of marital privacy and intimacy.

2. Trust promoted

The second aim of personal ministry is the building of faith, as expressed in *Romans 15.13*:

> 'Now the God of hope fill you with all joy and peace in believing, that ye may abound in hope, through the power of the Holy Ghost.'

This is a life of faith, and we are to be ever deepening in trust in God. Is someone very low, troubled or anxious? Then a soul needs to be encouraged to trust the Lord no matter what; to trust in his providential dealings, to commit his all to the Lord, and to pray for the strength to go through difficult situations. In mutual admonition we help each other not to fall into self-pity, grumbling and groaning, considering ourselves badly dealt with. We promote faith, for we are the Lord's, and know that he will not let things happen to us which we cannot deal with by his help. Through every situation of life he is training us, perhaps even chastising us, but he is at work, and we must trust him. The task of bringing one another to deeper trust, laying hold on the Lord, and praying and rejoicing in his love, is the second great objective of personal, mutual shepherding.

If only we can persuade one another of these things we will never be crushed, but able to say with the apostle: 'Troubled on every side, yet not distressed; we are perplexed, but not in despair … cast down, but not destroyed' *(2 Corinthians 4.8-9)*. No situation will destroy or corrupt our spiritual disposition and well-being while we walk by faith, bring all matters before the throne of grace, and trust him. The rule of Scripture is: 'Now the God of hope fill you with all joy and peace in believing, that ye may abound in hope, through the power of the Holy Ghost.'

3. Worship and reflection deepened

The third aim of mutual personal admonition is the promotion of sincere worship and reflection, referred to in *Romans 15.6*: 'That ye may with one mind and one mouth glorify God, even the Father of our Lord Jesus Christ.' Paul goes on to speak of God's promises that the Gentiles would praise him. We could refer again to *Colossians 3.16*, where the exhortation to mutual admonition flows into the use of hymns, psalms and spiritual songs.

Without doubt the promotion of the twin activities of worship and reflection should be a major aim of personal ministry. So much of the discomfort of believers may be relieved by worship and gratitude for all that God is, and for all that he has done. This is the way to lift up the soul and to trample down discouragement and difficulty. Thanksgiving, coupled with intelligent reflection on the ways and promises of God in the Word, and his past blessings to us, dispels more than anything else sadness, anxiety, and insecurity. Certainly it dispels vindictiveness, selfishness and worldliness. This is why worship should never be worldly in character, borrowing the polluted styles of worldly entertainment. Genuine worship is an antidote to all this, lifting the soul far above the self-centred, sin-centred thinking and emotionalism of a fallen world.

Is a believer angry with someone who has offended him? The answer is to engage in worship and praise to God for all his amazing kindness, and the unworthy anger will be shamed away. Self-pity withers and dies before a glorious Saviour, therefore we urge one another to reflective praise, thanksgiving and adoration. A good traditional book on worship would be worth a thousand counselling books, if it brought us to reflect personally and deeply on wonderful truths and sentiments in Scripture, as well as on hymns that sustain the blessing.

4. Scripture – for knowledge and happiness

Aim number four for personal ministry (though in importance this should be number one) is the study of the Bible, so that all may be 'filled with all knowledge' *(Romans 15.14)*. Paul emphatically identifies Scripture as the source of all comfort, saying, 'For whatsoever things were written aforetime *[the Old Testament]* were written for our learning, that we through patience and comfort of the scriptures might have hope' *(Romans 15.4)*. We therefore urge one another to be great learners, to read the Word of God, together with Matthew Henry, or whatever commentator helps our understanding. Believers should ideally have to hand a commentary which assists with difficult verses, such as Matthew Poole, who is one of the most concise of the Puritan commentators for resolving difficulties. One factor that sometimes impedes Bible study is the occurrence of verses that people simply don't understand, and such a work frequently resolves the difficulties in a few plain words.

Many years ago my wife and I frequently had tea with a very aged lady who would tax us to the limit, because she was always studying the Scripture. She would raise many interesting problems, saving them up for our visits. She would ask how one passage could be reconciled with another, and what this or that prophetic statement meant. We were often caught out by her astute questions, and it was clear that she was a great student of the Word, and that it kept her bright and alive and full of love for the Lord. It was her life to be studying the Word in her advancing years, and we would hope to be like her, great learners right to the end of life's journey.

Is someone inclined to be sad and troubled in their mind? There is no book that imparts happiness like the Word of God, sincerely studied. Even at a technical level it is so very wonderful, so consistent, so profound, and so comprehensive in scope. I have known many other people who have been great lovers and students of the Word, and whose grasp of its riches furnished and thrilled their minds and hearts through all the vicissitudes of life. It is so inspiring to interact with those who have been great learners of the Book divine throughout their earthly pilgrimage.

If we are crushed by life's burdens, tired of other people and of ourselves, spiritually cold and cast down, despairing of Heaven, overcome by some besetting sin, or overwhelmed by some problem, it is possible we have stopped feeding on the glorious Word of the living God. The authors of hordes of counselling books seem to think that they can do better than the Word of Life, but they have forsaken the fountain of living waters and hewn for themselves broken cisterns in the ever-shifting ground of human psychology. Their counsels take people away from reliance on the Lord, and from seeking joy in spiritual truth and blessing.

Therefore, our fourth aim is to be always promoting and stimulating the study and learning of God's Word and showing one another how it can be the source of knowledge, power, happiness and fulfilment for us all, in the service of God.

5. Sacrifice and service

Any treatment of the importance of sacrifice and service – our fifth aim – is generally absent from counselling books, yet the service of the Lord is central to the spiritual well-being of believers, for this is what we were saved for. In *Romans 15.16* Paul makes a seemingly mysterious statement, and speaks in an almost priestly manner, saying that God made him – 'the minister of Jesus Christ to the Gentiles, ministering the gospel of God, that the offering up of the Gentiles might be acceptable.' He seems to say, 'In evangelising Gentiles, I offer them up to God as a priest makes an offering at the altar.' He tells us what he means in chapter 12: 'I beseech you therefore, brethren, by the mercies of God, that ye present your bodies a living sacrifice, holy, acceptable unto God, which is your reasonable service.'

Gentiles are being won for the Lord to sacrifice themselves to his service, to live and witness for him, and be entirely at his disposal. This is the great fifth aim of all personal ministry, the urging of each other to be wholly offered up and given up to the Lord's service. We are intended to be the acceptable offering of the Gentiles. I hope readers will not find this overcritical, but I notice that the so-called mega-churches, mostly in the USA, which have hired professional counsellors, sometimes having teams of a dozen and more paid therapists, have a characteristic in common. The members of these churches seem to have no part in corporate service. If the church wants something done, they simply hire staff. They have ministers and other staff for everything. The members mostly attend only the morning worship, plus church concerts and banquets and so on, spending the best of their energies living comfortable, self-indulgent lives; indeed, one might say, mildly sanitised worldly lives. What matters is that family, house, car, education, college, and all these things must be as splendid as possible.

It is not surprising that such churches place so much emphasis on teams of paid therapists or counsellors. If – assuming they are truly converted – their lives were applied to the great goal of Christian service, their lives would be rich in spiritual fulfilment. They are missing the blessing of having serving priorities, answers to prayer, special upholding by the Lord, and fruit for his name. They are not what God meant them to be. If, as believers, our chief priority is the Lord's service, we forget about our aches and pains, offences, difficulties and problems, rejoicing in our calling and forgiving one another. I remember Dr Martyn Lloyd-Jones once saying that during the years of World War II, consultations with psychiatrists plummeted, because people had something greater to engage their minds than the pressures of everyday life. Similarly as believers, if our hearts are in the Lord's work, then our priorities are right. If evangelisation, children's Sunday School work, and other activities for Christ concern us, then we get all other matters in perspective, seeing them for what they are, and processing them with Christian calm.

If Christ comes first, then all other things fall into place, which is partly what the Saviour taught when he said: 'Therefore take no thought, saying, What shall we eat? or, What shall we drink? or, Wherewithal shall we be clothed? . . . But seek ye first the kingdom of God . . . and all these things shall be added unto you' *(Matthew 6.31-33)*. To encourage each other to live lives of sacrifice and service for the Lord is a vital aim of the ministry of admonition.

6. The outgoing, caring lifestyle advanced

This sixth aim of personal ministry – that we should press and urge one another to be an outgoing and caring people – is seen strongly in the words of *Romans 15.1-3*:

> 'We then that are strong ought to bear the infirmities of the weak, and not to please ourselves. Let every one of us please his neighbour for his good to edification. For even Christ pleased not himself; but, as it is written, The reproaches of them that reproached thee fell on me.'

The Puritan Richard Baxter's great cure for depression (or melancholy as it was then called) was to advise sufferers to do things for other people. If we were more outgoing as people, then we would be less susceptible to injury from woes and knocks. There are many people in our family circle, our church, and beyond who need encouragement from us. There are both children and elderly friends to care for, Christian workers to pray and provide for, newcomers in the church to befriend and assimilate – a never-ending list – beside the concern we have for lost souls. We should have no spare emotion for self-pity or emotional self-indulgence.

We recall what happened to the mother of the historic star of silent movies, Charlie Chaplin. This name is closely connected with the area around the Tabernacle, where Chaplin was born at the end of the 1880s. His father was a drunkard who abandoned his wife and boys. They lived in various rented rooms in little back streets behind the Kennington Park Road. Many are restored as lovely little houses now, but they were crumbling slums then. Their mother earned what she could through relentless labour, but they were desperately short. Although the boys knew about hunger they never starved, for it was their mother who starved, going without constantly. The lads were too young to quite realise what was going on, but the years of malnutrition later affected their mother's mind, and she was committed to a grim mental hospital. When the boys were adults, and successful, they took her to the United States, where she died, a very sick woman, in the 1920s. But here is the point. Mrs Chaplin was a regular worshipper at a Bible-believing church.

It was not the Tabernacle, I am thankful to say, but we cannot criticise the church because Christians can be very disappointing, and this can happen anywhere. She attended Christ Church, just opposite the Lambeth North underground station, which was then, of course, the church of F. B. Meyer. (Today it has lost its spiritual heritage, even denying the fundamentals of the faith.) Mrs Chaplin worshipped there, covering up as far as she could her poverty. The church folk did not realise that she had eaten nothing for days on end, but if anyone had been sensitive enough to notice this gaunt, emaciated lady, surely they would have grasped what was happening.

It is said that one of the reasons why Charlie Chaplin put up a barricade against God, was his resentment at how a church failed to help his mother, one of their regular worshippers. They took no notice. They did not seem to care about her. She was just one of the poor.

I mention this for our benefit. Are we 'depressed'? Then we should look out to help someone else! We should pray to God for a sensitive, outgoing heart to notice the needs of others, and draw alongside. Then we may just be able to put our pain to one side and help someone else at the same time. One of the great aims of personal counselling is 'to provoke unto love and to good works', and to be increasingly outgoing as a people. This is echoed in the appealing words of *Galatians 6.9-10*:

> '**Let us not be weary in well doing: for in due season we shall reap, if we faint not. As we have therefore opportunity, let us do good unto all men, especially unto them who are of the household of faith.**'

Modern counselling ministry books are all about us and our needs, whereas the Bible turns our gaze outwards, and makes us more Christ-like as people.

7. Friendship and cheer

Our concluding aim of inter-personal ministry is as fundamental and essential as the others – the duty of imparting friendship and cheer. As we are looking at *Romans 15* we will find this in the penultimate verse – verse 32: 'That I may come unto you with joy by the will of God, and may with you be refreshed.' It will be so good to be with you, Paul says, for it will cheer my heart no end, and refresh my spirit to have your fellowship, dear friends. We must be keen to urge one another to provide friendship and cheer; it is our duty, as well as a most uplifting activity. We say to husbands and wives at wedding services – you have a duty to cheer each other up. And we all have this duty, whether as friends or fellow-labourers. We have a duty to encourage and uplift those around us, and not to inflict upon them our heavy moods and despondent thoughts, let alone our complaints and miseries.

Forty-five years ago I knew a man who wished to be a pastor and to preach the Word, but he had a problem. He did not know how to smile, or at least I never saw him doing so. He had such an unlined face you imagined it would crack if he smiled. He was solemn to the point of gloominess, but if you asked, 'Aren't you happy?' he would insist that he was. He was happy appearing to be gloomy, and there are people who are like that, and often they do not realise how they appear to others. Like all of us, they must come to see that they have a duty to extend some cheer and warmth, especially as believers. This young man and I both knew an older lady who had spent her professional life training opera singers to present their voices. Having retired, she would give voice presentation advice to aspiring ministers. My friend went to see her, and she told him that his trouble was never smiling, and if only he smiled more, his face would become more elastic and his words would be better-presented. How can you be a pastor or a personal shepherd among believers, if you are inclined to depress people?

We have a duty to cheer others with genuine friendliness, with the things of God, and with the blessings that we have received. Increasing gas and electricity prices may well be mentioned between us, but such themes should never dominate our conversation. If it is necessary to mention negative matters, we should always be ready to mention also positive matters, because we are spreading happiness in the Lord. The old hymn of William Cowper we quoted earlier is seldom sung, but may profitably be often read because it makes the point so well. It is about prayer, but has these two verses which apply to the present point.

Have we no words, ah, think again!
Words flow apace when we complain
And fill our fellow-creature's ear
With the sad tale of all our care.

Were half the breath thus vainly spent
To Heaven in supplication sent,
Our cheerful song would oftener be,
'Hear what the Lord has done for me.'

There is a challenging proverb that says: 'A man that hath friends must shew himself friendly' *(Proverbs 18.24)*. It cuts two ways, the first meaning being this: if a person wants to have friends, he had better show himself friendly. But it can run the other way also, meaning: a person who has friends has a duty to be friendly to them also, or if he fails to pull his weight and return their goodness to him, he may even drive them away. The believer who is always needing and taking comfort and help will always need it, while the person who gives out friendship or cheer will be happy and fulfilled in doing so. And this is all the more true when it is done in the name of the Lord, and with his help and inspiration.

Here, then, are our seven aims for the ministry of mutual help and admonition, and they are so different from the complex human treatments of the modern counselling movement:–

1. Character – we are here to exhort one another to build character, with the Word of God in our hands.

2. Trust, prayer, faith – we are to encourage one another to pray and to exercise faith.

3. Worship and reflection – we are to encourage one another to worship with all our hearts, and practise constant thanksgiving.

4. Learning – we are to encourage one another to love and study the Word as our favourite pastime.

5. Sacrifice and service – we are to promote commitment to service for the Lord.

6. Outgoing and caring – we are to spread the blessedness of an outgoing, caring lifestyle.

7. Friendship and cheer – we are to give an example of, and promote in others, the practice of cheering up those around us.

Personal ministry is not playing at pseudo-psychoanalysis, and digging and delving into the lives of others. 'I myself also,' says Paul, 'am persuaded of you, my brethren, that ye also are full of goodness, filled with all knowledge, able also to admonish one another.'

7
The Defeat of Talebearing

'Thou shalt not go up and down as a talebearer among thy people'
(Leviticus 19.16).
'He that uttereth a slander, is a fool' *(Proverbs 10.18).*
'An hypocrite with his mouth destroyeth his neighbour' *(Proverbs 11.9).*

GOSSIP HAS BEEN DEFINED as idle talk or compulsive news-mongering, including the spreading of groundless rumour. It is not always hostile or malevolent, but this chapter focuses on the kind of gossip that complains about others behind their back, exposing their faults (or supposed faults) and pulling them down in the estimation of all who will listen. This is about the 'backbitings' and 'whisperings' mentioned in *2 Corinthians 12.20*.

We begin with a few comments about hopeless, persistent gossips. Some people – even some Christians – seem driven to negative gossip about others. The tendency within them has become so powerful that they can no longer control it. They are like alcoholics or drug addicts. They prowl like gunboats, their arsenals stacked high with derogatory information about different people, and their 'radio antennae' sensitive to the latest 'suspicious' situations. As Christians they are certainly in a very sad and sick state of mind, because spiritual interests and harmful gossip are mutually exclusive. It is obvious that their minds now draw their satisfaction from sordid things secretly spread. Gossips are undoubtedly backsliders, however consistent they may appear to be in attending meetings, and however vocal in claiming spiritual blessing.

How do some who are believers get into such a state? The forces behind gossip will be identified shortly, but it must be said that people who are inveterate gossips have obviously made no attempt to curb or fight their habit. They do not seem to have seen it as a sin, or to have detested and resisted it. Just as people given to temper tantrums allow their muscles of self-control to waste away, so also hopeless gossips become disastrously weak. They are to be blamed. This is a condition for which they are entirely responsible. It is self-induced.

Persistent gossips appoint themselves as judge and jury of other people, while they are the weakest and most pathetic. Self-control is one of the noblest human strengths, but gossips have none. The faculty of self-control (of the mind and the mouth) has capitulated to Satan. Only a divine operation can save inveterate gossips, and the Holy Spirit must be the Surgeon. Hopeless gossips, by full and sincere repentance to God, must submit to the sanctifying help of the Spirit, and the people of God must help by refusing to hear their gossip, nursing them back to spiritual priorities by the quality of their own conversation.

Repentant gossips must see themselves as people who – through persistent sin – have been left with a weakness or lameness like former alcoholics. They must recognise their tendency to fall into the sin of gossip, and they must not let a day pass without setting a watch on their lips and minds. Whenever the urge comes to run another person down, or to retail unpleasant 'facts', they must pray for help, summon all their strength to suppress the urge, and divert their thoughts to something wholesome and edifying. If they have given way to the gossiping urge for months or years, rehabilitation may be a long fight, but as they battle they will grow stronger. If they are not prepared to fight, they will rapidly slip back into utter hopelessness, creating havoc among God's people, and becoming candidates for the chastisement of the church and of the Lord.

The most frightening aspect of this topic is that *occasional* gossips are in very great danger of becoming continual, hopeless gossips. This is a habit that quickly spirals out of control, and rules the tongue. We turn now to the question – Why are people, even Christian people, tempted to gossip? What triggers the destructive urge? To consider the despicable causes serves as a kind of 'aversion therapy' to earnest and sensitive believers.

Ten causes of gossiping

'Keep thy tongue from evil, and thy lips from speaking guile' *(Psalm 34.13).*

First – the devil is the instigator of gossip. From the beginning he misrepresented the character of God in his dealings with Adam and Eve. He insinuated that God was unfairly withholding something from them, and was not truthful to them. He implied that God was unreasonable, even tyrannical toward them. Satan's words outwardly borrowed an element of truth, but they were not the truth. God had certainly withheld the knowledge of evil from Adam and Eve, but not for the reasons advanced by Satan. (Gossip is not always entirely untrue, but it misrepresents and distorts the truth until it is no longer true.) The devil is the father of malicious gossip, and first uttered it amidst the beauty of paradise. Ever since, he has reproduced his crime using co-operative people. Gossip is planted in the minds of believers by the father of lies.

Secondly – gossips may be motivated by envy, jealousy and pride.

Those tempted to gossip should look within themselves. Are they genuinely hurt and concerned by someone's wrong conduct, or is there a spirit of jealousy smouldering within? Do the victims of their gossip have advantages or blessings in life which cause jealous resentment? Do the victims have a degree of acceptance and fruitfulness which arouses the envy of gossips, who proudly think they should have these things? Jealousy and pride make virulent gossips.

Thirdly – gossips may be motivated by a general discontent with their lot, or may be suffering the result of personal failure. Instead of looking to God for help, and drawing on spiritual comforts, the gossip develops a complaining, bitter spirit, hitting out at others through malicious words. The devil is always on the watch for dissatisfied and vulnerable people through whom he may mount a whispering crusade against others.

Fourthly – gossip may be stirred by resentment. Perhaps at some time other Christians have brought necessary words of reproof to them, but they still rankle. To resentful people vengeance is sweet, and gossip is a 'knife shaped for the back'.

Fifthly – gossips are often motivated by a longing to be listened to. Pathetic as it sounds, some people feel that they can attract attention only by having something startling or discrediting to say about others. Gossips have discovered that many people (due to the fallen human heart) are powerfully attracted to their stories.

Sixthly – gossips are sometimes motivated by the absence of anything better to say. Unpleasant as it sounds they are people with empty heads. They cannot think of anything worthwhile to say, because they never read or talk about anything of substance. Apart from commenting on the weather, all they can do is criticise others. They are too insubstantial to be anything other than retailers of distorted, hostile stories.

Seventhly – people so often become gossips because they are worldly in their tastes and outlook. After all, gossip is the stuff of worldliness. Perhaps they are avid followers of television soaps, which are dramatised gossip administered in massive doses for addicts. If people watch serialised gossip, their attitudes and tastes are bound to be shaped by it. They will become inquisitive about the minute twists and turns of the lives of others, and especially about their failings and faults. They live in a world where human behaviour is everything, and spiritual behaviour is worth nothing. Here is the ideal mental training of a malicious gossip.

Eighthly – gossips are produced by the old disease of self-righteousness. One might say that the Pharisee (in the Lord's parable) who went into the Temple to pray, betrayed the marks of a gossip. He prayed with himself, denigrating the tax collector who stood nearby. By tearing down others, self-righteous people build up themselves. By slandering people in the church, the self-righteous gossip succeeds in promoting himself above them. He effectively convinces himself of his standing, and at the same time convinces others also. For self-righteous people, gossip is a ladder to self-satisfaction.

Ninthly – gossips may be motivated by sheer vindictiveness and malice. Some people do not need a reason for hating others, they just do. There is within them some primitive hostility which they do not attempt to control. They never seem to be challenged by the command of Christ that believers should love one another. They simply do not care if nastiness of character pours out of them. They allow it free rein and feel no shame. They need to see that there is a whole area of their conduct which has not been brought into the work of sanctification.

Tenthly (and closely linked with the previous point) – gossips will be encouraged in their sin by the abandonment of regular self-examination and repentance. If there is no self-review at the close of the day, and no pang of conscience and painful shame, there will be nothing to check the outflow of gossip. To curb the old nature and its sins requires conscientious concern. Complacency in this leads to a low view of the seriousness of gossip, and even to its justification. The devil will convince gossips that it is right and necessary to bring to light the 'misdemeanours' of others. Daily self-examination not only convinces people about the sin of gossip, but it also makes gossips more keenly aware of all their other sins. It then becomes impossible for them to go about denigrating other people. Gossiping is a proud activity, and daily self-examination and repentance dissolves pride.

* * *

Hopefully, the reading of this list of causes will put readers off any desire to gossip. They are surely the greatest antidote. If this is what drives it, we should recoil in alarm and disgust.

SIX DEADLY EFFECTS
1. Against God's standards for speech

The Lord's commands governing the speech of believers are plain, but malicious gossip disobeys them all. The words of a gossip are like a fountain (writes James) sending forth sweet water and bitter at the same time. The Lord's requirements for Christian speech are: 'first pure, then peaceable, gentle, and easy to be intreated, full of mercy and good fruits, without partiality, and without hypocrisy' *(James 3.17)*. 'Sound speech, that cannot be condemned' is the standard for believers *(Titus 2.8)*. Backbiting and whispering are clear marks of godlessness and lack of repentance *(2 Corinthians 12.20-21)*. Malice, in word as well as deed, is repeatedly condemned *(Ephesians 4.31; Colossians 3.8; Titus 3.3; 1 Peter 2.1)*. Slander is always to be rejected *(1 Timothy 3.11)*. Evil speaking is to be put away, along with bitterness, and replaced by kindness, tender-heartedness and forgiveness *(Ephesians 4.32)*.

Gossip is, of course, condemned utterly in the supreme expression of God's holy law given in the ten commandments: 'Thou shalt not bear false witness against thy neighbour' *(Exodus 20.16)*. The more specific words of God given through Moses should ring in the ears of every potential gossip – 'Thou shalt not go up and down as a talebearer among thy people' *(Leviticus 19.16)*. To gossip is to be in opposition to God and to his Word. It is to wilfully trample on the standards of the Lord.

2. Against the Spirit's work

Gossip is opposed to every aspect of the fruit of the Spirit as described in *Galatians 5.22-23*.

- It is against love, for it is an act of unkindness, even of hostility.
- It is against joy, because it destroys the happiness not only of the victim, but sometimes of the whole church, sowing and spreading a complaining, vindictive spirit.
- It is against peace (or unity), because it creates suspicion, fostering a critical atmosphere, and setting one against another.
- It is against longsuffering, pouncing on every perceived misdemeanour, and fermenting a spirit of anger and intolerance.
- It is against gentleness, being spiteful and hurtful in character, and possessing an insatiable appetite for 'offenders' to devour.
- It is against goodness, which refers to a magnanimous, generous, helpful spirit. Gossip, by contrast, gives no quarter and shows no leniency. Far from giving the benefit of the doubt, or helping the criticised person to recover, it moves in for the kill, and destroys the victim's character and reputation.
- It is against faithfulness to one another. Loyalty is the first casualty of gossip. The gossiping, backstabbing person feels and shows absolutely none.
- It is against meekness and humility, because gossips feel no need to be certain of the facts, nor are they inhibited by any sense of their own sinfulness. They are quite perfect in their own eyes. *Philippians 2.3* tells us that 'lowliness of mind' leads people to esteem others better than themselves. Gossip operates in the opposite direction.

- It is against temperance, or self-control, because gossips cannot contain themselves. They make no attempt to hold back their words, even though their habit is obviously evil, vicious, cowardly, and cruelly damaging.

Gossip is against every tenet and feature of Christian character, rendering sanctification impossible. It is against the improvement of the people it criticises, and it is against the spiritual growth of the gossips themselves. What a sin this is, to be capable of blighting *every single bloom* of the fruit of the Holy Spirit in the life of believers and in the life of the church! Who would be a gossip?

3. Against the whole church

Gossip is an act of hatred not only toward those criticised, but toward the whole fellowship of God's people, laying an axe to the root of brotherly love and union. Once its fever spreads, the words of James become true. 'And the tongue is a fire, a world of iniquity: so is the tongue among our members, that it defileth the whole body, and setteth on fire the course of nature; and it is set on fire of hell.'

Gossip, it must be remembered, is two diseases, not one. It is a disease of the mouth *and* a disease of the ears. The gossiper is not the sole offender. Every incident of gossip inflicts guilt equally on listeners. They receive the sin, perhaps relishing and enjoying it, making it their own. *Their* hearts are hardened toward the victim, and they so often become 'tellers' in their turn. To gossip is as treacherous as recruiting another person to lie or steal or cheat. It is against the victims, the hearers, and ultimately the whole church.

'A froward man soweth strife: and a whisperer separateth chief friends' *(Proverbs 16.28).*

4. Against truth

Gossip is against truth, in every sense of the word. First, it is against *biblical* Truth, because it takes the hearts and interests of people away from spiritual food, diverting them to earthly 'scandal'.

Wherever gossip is popular, believers lose their absorbing passion for the Word of God. 'For whereas there is among you envying, and strife, and divisions, are ye not carnal?' *(1 Corinthians 3.3.)* Could there be any greater tragedy than the sight of once-keen Christians who now go to God's house only to hear morsels of rumour and innuendo?

Gossip is also against truth in the sense that it is usually largely dishonest. It clutches hold of accusations and reports against others, and retells them without any attempt to check or verify the truth. Not only does gossip omit to check the facts, it invariably states them in the worst possible light, and embellishes and exaggerates them. The untruthfulness of gossip does not stop there. It operates behind its victim's back, concealing all sign of its activity. Should the victim bump into the gossip, forced, hypocritical smiles of friendliness hide the deed. Furthermore, gossips often feign a reluctance to speak about their victim, and make the untrue claim that they do so only out of concern for the 'offender'. The gossip thus becomes an actor or actress, but the whole performance is an appalling lie, and God sees. In every way, gossip is the enemy of truth.

5. Against order

Gossip is also disorderly, riding roughshod over the proper procedures given by the Lord for dealing with offences and misbehaviour in the church. For personal offences the Lord commands an honest, open, direct, personal approach, carried out in a right spirit (with meekness). For other offences pastors and officers have been given to the churches with clear and sensitive directions for overseeing the discipline and shepherding of the flock. For serious offences there is a revealed sequence of steps, including pleadings and warnings, and, for certain cases, even exclusion. Gossips, however, think they can dispense with the divine scheme in its entirety, and take the care of the church into their own hands. Viewed from God's perspective, their activities combine arrogance with disobedience, and violate the biblical procedures of the church, ordained for correction and restoration.

6. Against the Gospel

Finally, gossip is against the Gospel, because it steals from people their compassion and zeal for the souls of others, and grieves away the Holy Spirit, so that powerful, soul-saving work is hindered. 'Where envying and strife is,' says Scripture, 'there is confusion and every evil work.' Envying and strife is 'not from above, but is earthly, sensual, devilish' *(James 3.14-16)*. Do we indulge in gossiping? To see the ugliness of it and its effect upon the church ought surely to make us think, and put us off. We must neither speak gossip, nor listen to it.

Should we expose a gossip?

C. H. Spurgeon gave valuable counsel on how to subdue gossip. When someone comes to you with a string of complaints about another, he advises that we ask that person to put it all in writing. The perpetrator of gossip will not usually do this because it requires openness and truthfulness.

Suppose we know that serious gossip is circulating, injuring its victims and damaging the church fellowship. And suppose we cannot ourselves, for some reason, confront the gossips. Should we tell a church officer, perhaps the pastor? Should we 'report' the matter? Would this be a case of gossiping about the gossip? The answer is, that it would be our duty to God and the church. When there were troubles in the church at Corinth, members of Chloe's family told Paul, and he challenged the church. This was done in clear obedience to the rule of Christ, who said that when offences arise which cannot be solved between individuals, we must 'tell it unto the church' *(Matthew 18.17)*.

A gossip is both a terrorist and a wounded person. If we saw a seriously injured individual bleeding in the street, would we not call an ambulance? If we saw a terrorist planting a bomb on our church premises, would we not raise the alarm? Satan has at some time whispered into the ear of every believer a commandment of his own invention. We hear and we may accept it, even giving it pride of place above all the true commandments of the Lord. The pseudo-commandment we have in mind here is the idea that it is dishonourable to tell on anyone, no matter what that person has done. It is our duty, so we may think, to give the offender our total support and protection, and never betray him to the office bearers of the church. This notion is of Satan, not of God, and if the high crime of gossip proceeds to injure a fellowship, it is time for those who hear either to challenge the gossip, or to tell it to those who are charged with the peace and purity of the church.

> 'Wherefore laying aside all malice, and all guile, and hypocrisies, and envies, and all evil speakings' *(1 Peter 2.1).*

> 'Let all bitterness, and wrath, and anger, and clamour, and evil speaking, be put away from you, with all malice' *(Ephesians 4.31).*

> 'Nor revilers...shall inherit the kingdom of God' *(1 Corinthians 6.10).*

The opposite of all this is a hallmark of Christian character, so well expressed in Benjamin Keach's *Solemn Covenant* for his congregation of 1689:–

> 'We do solemnly promise to bear with one another's weaknesses, failings, and infirmities, with much tenderness, not discovering them to any without the church, nor any within, unless according to Christ's rule, and the order of the Gospel provided in that case.'

8
Closeness to God

The Assurances of *Psalm 139*

'O Lord, thou hast searched me, and known me' *(Psalm 139.1)*.

THERE ARE MANY great themes in this psalm such as the omniscience of God, his infinite knowledge of all things, his omnipresence and his omnipotence, or almighty power. Throughout the psalm run also the themes of the love of God, his care for his people, and thoughts of eternity. But this chapter will track King David's reflections – throughout the psalm – of God's closeness to him. Of this comforting sign of spiritual life and being, the king was convinced.

For all who have come to Christ, trusting in him and his atoning death, closeness to God is a reality, though it is not always perceived by sense, as Newton's (original) hymn says –

Though sometimes unperceived by sense,
Faith sees him always near.

When not perceived by a sense of assurance, or by outward

evidence of his blessing, God's presence may always be embraced by reflection on all that the Scripture says about his closeness to his people. We may draw our comfort from the Scriptures and also from our experience of his mighty acts within us and towards us.

There is never a tangible touch or physical sensation of God's presence with us, for we know him by faith. There is, however, an inner certainty imparted to us that God is our God, that his Word is true, and that those who have trusted in him are his, but this conviction is not necessarily a continuous experience. Many times the clouds may roll across the heavens, and the 'feelings system' ceases to operate, and then we walk by faith in God's Word and promises. However, if we only look, there is always a river of evidence running through our lives of the Lord's operation in us. At those times when assurance sags, it is by reflection that we recover peace, and this psalm of David gives so much scope for our thought.

Verse 1

'O Lord, thou hast searched me, and known me.'

Verse one takes the form of a prayer to God. The word used for 'search' is a strong one, meaning to cut deeply into something to examine the inside. Of course God knows all things without a laboured search. We hold in our mind at any time only a tiny proportion of the facts we know, but God knows everything consciously, past, present and future, all the time. He has an infinite eternal knowledge, and nothing is concealed from him.

We are also 'searched' for our conduct and our sin; for God sees it all. As the king reflects on this, he is overwhelmed by the realisation of God's might and majesty, and his own accountability. How much he has been forgiven! How vast is God's mercy and kindness toward him! So much sin has been carried away and lost in the kindly seas of God's everlasting forgetfulness, and the Lord has loved him notwithstanding all. The Lord has also seen the king's every thought, every fear, and every need, and takes account of everything for his care.

Does he need discipline, or comfort, or strength? Does he require deliverance from a situation which is more than he can cope with? God knows all, and in his wisdom responds to the king's cries. The Lord may appear to hold back until he is called upon, because that is what David must do, but he knows everything.

The phrase 'and known me' is not just repetition. It means, as it so often does in both Old and New Testaments, that God has established a relationship with his child, having set his love upon him, and determined never to leave him nor forsake him.

Verse 2

'Thou knowest my downsitting and mine uprising.'

Verse two plainly tells us that God knows all our needs, actions and words when we are active and busy, functioning professionally, and also when we are at ease or at home. God knows, for example, if we are living two lives, an outer public life, which is better controlled and ordered than our home life. At church or in the workplace we may be greatly appreciated, but at home we may prove unhelpful, unkind, uninterested in our spouse or children, and unsympathetic. It is a sad thing over 50 years of pastoring to have seen some seemingly fine people who have let themselves down badly in their other place, and have moved into grotesque hypocrisy. To be aware that God's eye is upon us in our downsitting and uprising, convicts and challenges us to consistent genuineness in our living. Equally the verse searches the two sides of our spiritual life – our outward faithfulness of worship and service, and our secret inner life of prayer. Are they alike in fervour and application?

The second half of verse two – 'Thou understandest my thought afar off' – is about those times when we have no strong sense of God. He is not in our mind. We may be distracted by earthly duties and concerns so that our sense of God has deserted us and we feel no strong assurance. It is hard to pray because we feel so far removed. At such a time we must pray with our mind alone, at a purely intellectual level, because the heart and feelings will not co-operate. The verse assures us that this is wholly acceptable to God. Many divines have suggested that God values this kind of prayer more highly than any other because it involves faith alone. We may always call upon him with the mind alone, praise, thank and worship him, even though feeling and assurance are disabled. He is the same even if we are not, and even as we call upon him in such a condition, our assurance is often restored to us. We see that happening in several of David's psalms.

Verse 3

> 'Thou compassest my path and my lying down, and art acquainted with all my ways.'

The Hebrew of verse three says, 'Thou winnowest my path.' When grain is winnowed the air fills with dust and fragments, and the idea in this verse is that God surrounds us in the same way with the cloud of his presence. Even though we may be off the track of spiritual obedience, God is still observing, and has us in mind. Even when we are to blame, he knows how and by what means he will convict, chastise perhaps, and bring us back to restoration.

The second half of the phrase, 'Thou compassest my path and my lying down,' perhaps indicates that at times when we are exhausted or overwhelmed, or crushingly disappointed in ourselves, God is still compassing us about.

The phrase, 'And art acquainted with all my ways', provides a towering incentive to holiness and carefulness, compelling us to look to him in everything. This sense of being under God's eye is among the hallmarks of Christian character.

Verse 4

> 'For there is not a word in my tongue, but, lo, O Lord, thou knowest it altogether.'

Of course God knows everything we say, but verse four indicates that God knows every word before we say it. He knows all the things we meant to say or wanted to say, but were too timid to say. He knows what we nearly said, and all our bad reactions, ill-tempered responses, excuses and dishonest words, for 'There is not a word in my tongue but, lo, O Lord, thou knowest it altogether.' He knows those unspoken words and the motive lying behind them.

On the positive side, God knows all the right and truthful and good and gracious things that we say, and he will bless us for them. No good word of edification, comfort, encouragement or helpfulness goes unnoticed and unrewarded *(Matthew 5.43-48)*.

Verse 5

'Thou hast beset me behind and before, and laid thine hand upon me.'

The sentiment of verse five meant much to David, for God had closed him in and would not let him throw himself away. Several times in his life David acted in a way that was entirely uncharacteristic of his essential godly character, seemingly throwing himself off the right path of obedience to the Lord. But he is able to say that because he is truly the Lord's, and knows and loves him, the Lord will not let him destroy himself by impulsive sin. He closes him in: 'Thou hast beset me behind and before.' We know about his sin with Bathsheba, and his later indulgence towards Absalom. Perhaps, also, as a great general, he might have been tempted to go too far, pursuing acquisition of land for his own kingly glory. There must have been many temptations, but God would intervene, and what an assurance this was to him, and to us also. God will not let us go too far in the wrong direction, forward or backward, for his hand is laid upon us; his preventing, disciplining, correcting, strengthening, steadying hand.

His guidance also is real, when we call upon him. Some of today's evangelical writers say that there is no such thing as Christian guidance, but they are very greatly mistaken. The Bible teaches that God has a will for our life, and he will guide his people and lead them if they sincerely put themselves at his disposal and pray for wisdom.* The closeness of God to his people includes the outworking of his sovereign purpose in each life.

Verse 6

'Such knowledge is too wonderful for me; it is high, I cannot attain unto it.'

The term 'wonderful' in verse six refers to something too difficult to discern. God's dealings with his people are so high and great and intricate that they cannot be fully understood. Some events we may see the purpose of, while the meaning of others we understand more as time unfolds. One day we shall see fully how God was guiding our life, superintending, disciplining, and adding to us. Overall, however, our experience is too wonderful to chart. We cannot examine or discern everything. Some people are able to take a car or other machine to pieces, and reassemble it without error, but none of us can entirely analyse God's direction of our course. We only have insights from time to time. 'It is high, I cannot attain unto it.' It is higher than anything on earth.

Very few people can say a queen or prime minister takes a close interest in them, comes to their rescue, guides their affairs, and picks up the pieces when they go wrong. But though lowly in the eyes of the world, we can say that the King of kings and Lord of lords is directing our affairs. This is 'high' knowledge, higher than any situation seen on earth. 'I cannot attain unto it.'

Usually it is best that life's pathway is not an open book to us. If we knew where God was taking us, we might recoil from going down that path. We might shrink from God's training plan for our future. It is for the best that we do not see everything, but we do

---

* *Steps for Guidance* by Peter Masters, published by Wakeman Trust, defends and explains the seeking of guidance.

see many, many extraordinary preparations and provisions in our unfolding lives, and innumerable answers to prayer along the way, and we know that we, astonishingly, live in the heart of the Triune Godhead and his eternal purpose.

Verse 7

'Whither shall I go from thy spirit? or whither shall I flee from thy presence?'

Verse seven is a magnificent verse. It may be the psalmist has in mind wandering from the track again. Perhaps he longs to escape from some correction that God had laid upon him. It cannot be accomplished, he says, for we are always in God's sight and in his care. The Lord of lords is never absent and his plan for us will ultimately stand. Pardon and renewing grace are only ever a prayer away, and our heavenly destination remains unchanged.

Verse 8

'If I ascend up into heaven, thou art there: if I make my bed in hell, behold, thou art there.'

Verse eight gives some possibilities, 'If I ascend up into heaven, thou art there.' This is not to be read merely as poetry, as if the king intended to say that God's power and influence knows no bounds. It is not just about the omnipresence and immense nature of God, though that is implied, of course. David speaks of his dying and going to Heaven, where God is, and where he fills all in all. He will go to the paradise of Christ.

But in the case of an unconverted person whose body goes into the grave (the Hebrew refers to the place of the dead), it is not the end, for he is still accountable to God, and must go to judgement.

David, however, may have in mind wilful backsliding, when a believer makes his bed in hell by going back into the world, a kind of metaphorical hell. God will be there, and the believer will be disciplined, chastised perhaps, and turned back, by his great goodness.

Verses 9-10

'If I take the wings of the morning, and dwell in the uttermost parts of the sea; even there shall thy hand lead me, and thy right hand shall hold me.'

Verse nine speaks of east and west, the wings of the morning being a metaphor for the rising of the sun. Here is the sun rising in the east and setting in the west, the longest journey possible. Even there (verse ten) 'shall thy hand lead me, and thy right hand shall hold me'. The right hand of God denotes his ownership and supreme control of us, his leading of us. Our security is in his hand.

When far out of familiar surroundings of home or office, the Lord is our strength, support, and closest friend. When assailed by unexpected, never-before-encountered trials, he is there. If whirled away by war and conscription, and plunged into an unknown environment, he is there. If bereaved and forsaken, he is near. This is the experience of God's people throughout the world in every generation – never left alone by God, but always upheld and uplifted in answer to prayer.

Verse 11

'If I say, Surely the darkness shall cover me; even the night shall be light about me.'

Verse eleven extends the relieving power of God to a range of possible trials. For David these would have included events during his pursuit by Saul, and many other occasions that, humanly, would bring one to despair. For us the problem could be the impenetrability of an unbelieving community or the implacable atheism of all in the office, or extreme opposition to witness and faith within the family. Or there may be a trial by depression or loss of assurance, or strange and strong doubts of salvation.

At Hachilah David had experienced the most remarkable deliverance from Saul, and yet a sudden despair and despondence came over him, and he became sure he would now perish by the hand of

Saul. Convinced it was the end of his hope of the kingdom, he fell to desperation and despair. But at length, in time, the night would become light about him, and this is the unfailing outcome for us all, as we trust our Lord, and cry to him.

Verse 12

'Yea, the darkness hideth not from thee; but the night shineth as the day: the darkness and the light are both alike to thee.'

Verse twelve has a curious statement – 'Yea, the darkness hideth not from thee.' This does not simply mean that God can see in the darkness. Darkness is personified, as though it tries to hide, like a spiritual enemy. It seeks to hide its wretched work from God, but it cannot do so, as God sees it forming and can dismiss it in a moment if he chooses. 'But the night shineth as the day: the darkness and the light are both alike to thee.' God indeed sees every initiative of Satan and his host, and every hostile scheme or slander of men designed to hurt or discredit believers, and is ready to frustrate, limit or curtail them according to his will, and with regard to how much he will permit us to be assailed.

Verses 13-16

'For thou hast possessed my reins: thou hast covered me in my mother's womb. I will praise thee; for I am fearfully and wonderfully made: marvellous are thy works; and that my soul knoweth right well. My substance was not hid from thee, when I was made in secret, and curiously wrought in the lowest parts of the earth. Thine eyes did see my substance, yet being unperfect; and in thy book all my members were written, which in continuance were fashioned, when as yet there was none of them.'

Another train of thought is found in verses 13-16. 'For thou hast possessed my reins.' Literally, this means that God takes possession of my kidneys, a metaphor for our innermost feelings or desires. 'Thou hast covered me in my mother's womb.' From conception God's hand is upon David, and upon all who belong to Christ, in a special way. God determined exactly what genes we would have, what characteristics, powers and capacities we would bear. It was not open to view, it was his secret work – 'My substance was not hid from thee, when I was made in secret [not fashioned by human hands, not observed], and curiously wrought [with great skill] in the lowest parts of the earth.'

As if in the lower parts of the earth, deep underground, out of sight, secretly performed, a child is formed in the womb. God directs and determines all. 'Thine eyes did see my substance, yet being unperfect; and in thy book all my members were written, which in continuance were fashioned [were subsequently fashioned and shaped], when as yet there was none of them.' They were in the book of God in the design that God intended. He predetermined who we would be. God did his secret work, and then brought forth the noblest creation, a child, a man, a woman, with distinctive features, many of which in their various combinations would belong to that child alone, perhaps exclusively throughout the history of the world.

Before conversion, we do not understand this. Although he gave us our distinctive characteristics, we gave him no thanks and we felt no indebtedness. We underestimated the sophistication of this structure, this creation brought into the light of day. But after conversion, we see how much we owe, both for birth and for second birth especially. We marvel at our previous blindness to these things, and fall before him in praise and wonder.

Several verses are given to this theme and the picture is built up – marvellously wrought, out of sight, and then brought forth, a child for God. Here is King David's exposition of God's predestinating love, and of God's close identification and interest in his children.

Verse 17

'How precious also are thy thoughts unto me, O God! how great is the sum of them!'

Verse 17 reflects – How precious are God's many, many thoughts towards his children. The Hebrew says how 'heavy', which implies precious like gold, weighty and valuable. Every thought of God towards us will accomplish something substantial and eternal for us, for our good, and for his service and honour. Every thought (or counsel, or determination) contains by our standards a thousand other subordinate thoughts, they are so deep and full of matter.

The beautiful phrase 'how great is the sum of them' refers not only to their number, but to their degree of co-ordination. All thoughts of God toward us work together – 'all things work together for good'. The thoughts of God are a vast tapestry, interlocking, interweaving countless strands of events and influences towards us throughout life. How often we should reflect on God's work in our lives, to bring glory to him, and to lift our spirits and our thanksgiving! That was clearly the practice of the king.

Verse 18

'If I should count them, they are more in number than the sand.'

This verse concludes the seam of thought, declaring that the acts of God towards us, his answers to prayer, his unasked-for blessings and helps, and his deliverances that flood over us day by day, are so numerous they cannot be listed. They cannot possibly all be remembered. If, therefore, we do not thank him for today's blessings, he will never receive adequate thanks for them. Ultimately the deficit of praise will be so great that we will never be able to thank him enough. God's thoughts are so numerous and magnificent, and our thanksgivings are so poor in return, we must return thanks while they are fresh in our minds, in the spirit of the hymn –

> *I'll praise my Maker while I've breath;*
> *And when my voice is lost in death*
> *Praise shall employ my nobler powers:*
> *My days of praise shall ne'er be past,*
> *While life and thought and being last,*
> *Or immortality endures.*

What we need to pursue in order to maintain awareness of the closeness of God, is more praise and more thanksgiving. This both seals and illuminates our closeness to God. We do not need sensations, tinglings or curious physical experiences when we have so much to lift us up and assure us.

9
Spiritual Happiness

'A merry heart maketh a cheerful countenance: but by sorrow of the heart the spirit is broken' *(Proverbs 15.13)*.

ONE OF THE great hallmarks of Christian character is a settled state of happiness in the Lord that continues even alongside times of grief, disappointment, oppression and illness. 'Rejoice in the Lord alway' says the apostle Paul, who endured so many trials and setbacks. 'Be content' echoes the writer of *Hebrews*. In *Proverbs* we find inspired utterances about the maintaining of spiritual happiness designed to keep us securely in the realisation of and thankfulness for all the riches of salvation.

A great sequence of verses before us in *Proverbs 15* has spiritual happiness as a common thread. To prepare for these verses we need to consider three proverbs in chapter 14, for these are mighty nuggets of wisdom that provide a perfect introduction.

Proverbs 14.10 reads: 'The heart knoweth his own bitterness; and a stranger doth not intermeddle* with his joy.' This remarkable statement tells us that each individual's heart alone feels its pain, and no one can share it well enough to relieve it. The message is that 'therapeutic sharing' is not greatly effective. Both lines of the proverb intertwine, so that we cannot intermeddle with either the joy or sorrow of another person. This may seem unproductive and negative, but it prepares us for the biblical way of understanding spiritual joy, and recovering it should it be lost.

It has become very fashionable to think that we can resolve one another's times of heaviness by deep sharing, and in some churches people get together in a kind of group therapy session, and share their pain. Undoubtedly, some help may be derived from sympathy and identification, but these can never, according to this proverb, be a *substantial* means of helping one another, even less a cure. True biblical counselling, as we shall see in the verses before us, does not simply say, 'Let me try and share this burden.' It says, 'This is what you need to do in order to be helped by the Lord.' It then gives a biblical procedure for dealing with times of difficulty and pain, urging us to reflect on Christ's work and purposes. It teaches us how to reflect, and warns us about putting our trust in sympathy, however helpful it may be, up to a point. Some people think deep sharing leads to catharsis, by which they hope pain escapes, and indeed it may, temporarily and superficially, but not deeply, because we cannot 'intermeddle' with another's deepest feelings.

A second introductory gem appears in *Proverbs 14.13*, which reads: 'Even in laughter the heart is sorrowful; and the end of that mirth is heaviness.' Plainly, laughter is no long-term cure for heaviness or sorrow. 'Light' sorrow, which everyone has from time to time, may dissipate with laughter, but deeper heaviness will soon resettle. The proverb says that even in laughter, the heart really remains heavy and sorrowful. Laughter, therefore, may appear to give temporary

---

* The Hebrew word means – braid, trade, mix or barter.

relief, but we need something better than this.

A third introductory proverb is *Proverbs 14.30*: 'A sound heart *[the Hebrew means a "well" heart]* is the life of the flesh: but envy the rottenness of the bones.' In other words, heaviness can never be eased by the pursuit of what other people have, such as wealth, possessions, power or esteem. To ache with desire will only make matters worse, yet this is often seen as a solution. The opposite of a sound heart, in this proverb, is a discontented heart, susceptible to envy, and this gives rise to a deep, internal pain which destroys spiritual loyalty, vigour, and strength. Only when the heart is at peace, and secure and contented, will it give rise to vigour and strength in our whole disposition.

These introductory proverbs supply three principles. Firstly, we must not think that heaviness, disappointment, or sorrow can be effectively lifted by sharing (helpful though that may be). Secondly, we must not think that laughter, or some amusing distraction such as escape into entertainment, will shift the problem. Thirdly, we must avoid 'wanting', and desire a sound heart, which is secure and contented, because only this will really help. With these in mind, we go on to *Proverbs 15.13*, where a whole group of verses speak about happiness.

1. The duty of happiness

Proverbs 15.13 reads: 'A merry heart *[the Hebrew means a "bright" heart]* maketh a cheerful countenance.' A cheerful countenance clearly stands for the entire disposition of a person. The proverb continues: 'but by sorrow of the heart the spirit is broken', which means 'whipped'. This asserts that the person will lose all taste for spiritual things, and assurance will disappear. The implied counsel of the verse is – you must have a happy heart! But this sounds like secular 'positive thinking'. Surely the Word of God rises higher than this? Positive thinking says – you must learn to be happy; you must train yourself to think positively and to look on the bright side. But biblical thinking is quite different from this. Secular positive thinking focuses on building up ourselves in self-confidence and self-sufficiency, and learning how to look at all our earthly aspirations as if they really can and will be accomplished by us. What is advised in the Bible, however, points to a different basis for the believer's happiness, namely that we should look away from ourselves and worldly things, and reflect on the Lord, and his sufficiency, and on the spiritual blessings that we have through the love and work of such a Saviour.

This proverb *(15.13)* really says: 'You have a duty to be happy in salvation and spiritual things.' A happy heart makes a cheerful person, but if we perpetually give hospitality to painful and sorrowful matters, our spirit will be whipped, humiliated and broken. Paul says, 'Rejoice in the Lord alway.' How do we do this? We reflect on the amazing, astonishing love of God towards his people. We reflect frequently on the incomprehensible price that was paid for worthless people like us. We reflect on the security of the believer, 'once in him, in him for ever'. We reflect on our experience of salvation, remembering what the Lord did in our lives when he turned us around, and blessed us beyond measure.

We reflect on all the evidences of God's favour that we have had in our pilgrimage, and his countless interventions in our affairs. Even when we have passed through deep waters, there have been so many instances of answered prayer, and of blessing. We think of the Lord's infinite power, and of how he has undertaken to see us through. We think of his unassailable promises, of future things, and of the glorious hereafter. We contemplate Christ and his majestic virtues. We survey all the understanding we have been given since the time when we knew nothing at all. Yet now we 'know all things', including the meaning of life and the ultimate purpose of all that we experience. These are priceless blessings, and when we appreciate these things, engaging in wholehearted praise and thanksgiving, the heart is strengthened even in the midst of trouble, and our entire disposition is changed. We must think about these things, and also read about them every day, privately and in public worship, glorifying God for such unsurpassable blessings, and expressing praise with every ounce of our being. We must go on to tell the Lord we will gladly submit to him, accepting his providential hand in our lives (without complaint), and undertaking to accept the challenges which future days will bring. These are our duties when in trouble, and in carrying them out we receive a joy that lives alongside understandable grief. Heaviness can no longer overwhelm us or swallow us up.

But what if a deep-seated grief comes into us, as it sometimes may, which cannot be shifted whatever we do or think? No matter how we reflect, it will not go. It is so obdurate and so internal it somehow seems to be embedded in our very substance. What should we do? The answer of *Proverbs* is that we should seek to contain it by the same means that we have just described. Even if, for a while, we may have to carry it, we must endeavour to limit it by exactly the same procedure. We certainly must not feed it. Should this grief or heaviness suggest to the mind all kinds of sorrowful things, we must refuse to fuel it by murmuring, sorrowing or lamenting. We should be determined to ration our thinking about grievous matters, and pray to God for help. Reflection and worship may not remove the most deeply entrenched heaviness, but they will limit and contain it, enabling us to keep Christian contentment, peace and trust alive alongside it. By this means we live in the spirit of *Isaiah 50.10*, the classic Puritan verse for believers under grievous affliction, 'Who is among you that feareth the Lord, that obeyeth the voice of his servant, that walketh in darkness, and hath no light? let him trust in the name of the Lord, and stay upon his God.'

2. Preventive medicine is important

Subsequent verses in *Proverbs 15* introduce different aspects of the route to spiritual happiness, verse 14 saying: 'The heart of him that hath understanding seeketh knowledge: but the mouth of fools feedeth on foolishness.' At first sight this verse seems to have no connection with spiritual happiness, but it is sandwiched between two verses that do, and is therefore on the same theme. Out of this group of thirteen verses, ten of them clearly address some component of spiritual joy, and the three that do not are obviously to be accommodated to the same subject. We will take verse 14 not merely as an observation, but as an exhortation, and assume it is a piece of preventive medicine.

When we feel happy in the Lord, and are not going through deep waters, this verse tells us what we should do in order to be strengthened for harder seasons. If you are wise, says the verse, you will pursue knowledge, or more specifically, discernment. Our trouble is sometimes that we only want to listen to this kind of counsel when we desperately need it, but precautions should be taken to safeguard against the problem. 'The heart of him that hath understanding [discernment] seeketh knowledge.' We must read the Word more studiously, and also spiritual and doctrinal books, extend our knowledge of the faith, learn about the history of God's people and triumphs of faith in times of trouble. Then when the testing times come, we shall be strong and prepared. The foolish believer, however, feeds his mind too much on trivial things, and then has no depth when troubles come.

3. Achieving a happy underlying state

Proverbs 15.15 opens to us a most profound insight into happiness and sadness, establishing a basic and vital principle. 'All the days of the afflicted are evil [that is, harmful or hurtful]: but he that is of a merry [happy] heart hath a continual feast.' Both parts of the proverb speak of something which is continuous. Happiness or misery, we learn, are actually continuous states. This is not the way we generally think about these two states; in fact we recoil from this view. We say that sometimes we are 'up' and sometimes 'down'. There is no continuous emotion. But this proverb asserts that whichever is the prevailing condition is actually our continuous state, our prevailing characteristic. We are either persistently gloomy, knowing only passing times of happiness, or we are generally contented and happy. The unhappy person never seems to rise above it, unless something happens to distract his attention for a while. His true and settled condition is one of unhappiness. He resembles the person who has an illness that is incurable, and who has good days and bad days. When he feels a little better, he does not imagine the illness has gone, but knows his symptoms will soon resume.

To see this spurs us on to take this matter seriously. We thought we just went up and down, but if we see we are negative, gloomy and unhappy people as our chief characteristic, then we will want to follow the spiritual remedies to transfer to the other side of the proverb, by the help of God, so that our prevailing attitude is one of happiness in the things of God. We may then know low and gloomy times, but they will only be phases. Our prevailing disposition will be one of happiness.

The counsel behind this proverb is to make that transfer, and the key is in the statement that the person who has a happy heart 'hath a continual feast'. If this is our condition, it is because we constantly see those rich aspects of Christ's love and person and work previously referred to. The 'meat and drink' of God is always available to us. Perplexing and disappointing things will continue to weigh us down, for even the Saviour wept over human suffering, but our prevailing condition should be that we deeply appreciate the Lord, his blessings, and his mission in the world.

4. The Lord must have first place

Proverbs 15.16 gives us a rule of life essential for the happy heart, namely, that the Lord himself must be our first and greatest desire. 'Better is little with the fear of the Lord than great treasure and trouble *[the Hebrew is "turmoil"]* therewith.' The counsel of this proverb is – never elevate your earthly objectives and benefits above your love for the Lord. Your earthly aims may be perfectly legitimate: things you need. Make sure they are reasonable and appropriate things, but, says the proverb, never fix or feast your mind on the desirability and pleasantness of these things, at the expense of your love for the Lord. Always maintain at fullest fervour your esteem for him, your personal devotions, your learning of him, and your witness and service for him, because he is the centre and purpose of your life.

If we let the Lord slip down our scale of priorities and admiration, we will quickly be absorbed by earthly and personal desires, and according to the proverb we will reap turmoil. Spiritual happiness, in this proverb, pivots on the very first word: 'better'. It is far, far better to have great reverence for Christ, with few possessions, than to have great wealth and a small Saviour. So we are to limit the time and attention we give to planning home decorations, choosing of car and appliances, clothing and entertainment. We shall give due attention to these things, of course, but if they become too important, they do so at the expense of Christ our Lord, and our spiritual contentment and happiness.

5. Fellowship is designed to help

Proverbs 15.17 runs along the same track as verse 16, yet deals with a distinctive aspect, presenting a picture of fellowship: 'Better is a dinner of herbs *[vegetables]* where love is, than a stalled ox *[a fattened ox, suggesting feasting]* and hatred therewith.' Whether the scene is of travellers on the road, or an ordinary homestead, there may be excellent companionship. Better is a simple dinner of vegetables among poorer people, where there is real community, than a great feast among people who have nothing in common, or who may be alienated family members or bitter rivals. Better to have simple fellowship with the Lord's people, than to be rich worldlings without bonds of understanding and the kindred ties of the new nature.

Our interests are so different from those of the worldling. If the Lord directs, we are happy to have little in this world. Certainly, we may be guided to be managing directors or highly placed in some other way, but this is not what we most value in life. Second to Christ, our priority is fellowship with the Lord's people. Verse 16 effectively says we must put the Lord first, and communion with him, and verse 17 says that kinship and love between fellow-believers is the next most valuable blessing to us. Both proverbs provide ground rules for happiness, and believers certainly need the comfort and encouragement (and mutual admonition) of the spiritual family.

6. Self-control is vital to happiness

Proverbs 15.18 identifies a quality essential to our fellowship with God and one another. 'A wrathful man *[who cannot control his feelings, and reacts instantly and angrily to matters]* stirreth up strife: but he that is slow to anger appeaseth strife.' Our relationship with others depends so much on how we control ourselves, and this applies not only to ill-tempered behaviour, but proneness to offence that smoulders behind forced smiles and feigned civility. This proverb has in mind quarrels and ill-feeling towards others, but it also refers to *strife within ourselves.* So often anger is not released in words, but it burns within, wrecking our communion with God, and our own happiness. What are we like? Are we over-sensitive and disagreeable? Do we readily entertain critical thoughts about others? If shocked or offended in some way, do we pause and reflect, controlling our feelings and balancing the other person's virtues against the supposed offence? Or do our thoughts rampage to and fro across these unhappy events and situations, stirring up anger and contempt within ourselves?

There is even a tragic, fearful and dangerous possibility that believers may get angry with the Lord – a state of affairs that used to be called a 'contention with the Lord'. This occurs when we bemoan our lot or situation so much that we effectively murmur against the Lord who has ordered our life and circumstances according to his perfect wisdom and love. As Christians we would never dare to address the Lord directly saying, 'You have been unfair to me; you have been unreasonable and unkind; you have lost sight of me.' But our resentment of our circumstances has an ugly and insolent eloquence before God, and unless we control ourselves, reflect, and gladly bow to his providential will, we shall forfeit blessing and forgo spiritual happiness. How much better to put those complaining thoughts to death and go back to verse 13 – thinking of what Christ means to us, and what he has done for us. If only we approached our perceived troubles in the right way, they would be turned to our eternal and spiritual good.

Therefore, let us not be easily angered either with others, or within ourselves, or with the Lord. Be careful to control proud, angry, testy reactions to circumstances, for this is vital for fellowship with God, and spiritual happiness. If any believer has a deep-seated problem with anger, there is a powerful, even invincible measure to put alongside conscious self-control, and that is prayer. For the anger problem, nothing succeeds like earnest prayer for deliverance.

7. Laziness destroys happiness

Proverbs 15.19 is another of the minority verses in the passage that does not seem to involve happiness, but in reality it does. 'The way of the slothful man is as an hedge of thorns: but the way of the righteous is made plain.' No one would deny that a path invaded and overgrown by a vicious thorn-hedge would be a painful experience. Laziness, says the proverb, turns the road of spiritual happiness into an arduous, miserable route. The principle is that happiness and laziness are mutually exclusive elements of the spiritual walk. It should seem obvious that if we fail to engage in devotions, and show no striving for holiness, and have no witness and service for the Lord, we shall have no warm assurance, and no blessed fulfilment.

In contrast, the proverb reads: 'The way of the righteous is made plain.' 'Righteous' could well be rendered 'diligent', for it clearly means here the opposite of slothful. This describes the person who is ardent in private and personal devotions, as well as other spiritual duties. He is also fair in taking his share of spiritual labour in the church. The *KJV* margin offers this translation: 'The way of the righteous is raised up as a causeway.' Here is a great highway raised up on an embankment, out of the drifting sand (or rampant thorns), providing an obvious and clear route. Do we skip devotions and never engage in self-examination and the putting to death of sin? Do we read a couple of verses daily without thinking much about them? Are we mechanical and brief in prayer?

Are we unnecessarily inconsistent at weeknight meetings, or seldom to be seen pulling our weight in the various ministries of the church? The hand of the Lord will undoubtedly be withdrawn from us in some measure, and our pathway will be full of thorns. All manner of trials will irritate us, and hinder us in the walk of faith. The picture here is of life on the farmstead of *Proverbs*. One of the sons on the farm is lazy and will not work or try hard at anything, and so he is always in trouble with his venerable father and everyone else in general. Spiritual indolence certainly impedes happiness in the spiritual realm.

8. A conscious desire to please God leads to happiness

Proverbs 15.20 expands the thought of laziness or diligence, adding a new element to the way of happiness. 'A wise son maketh a glad father: but a foolish man despiseth his mother.' Here are the parents and their two sons on a farmstead. One makes the father very glad because he learns well, applies all that he learns, and works hard. The other son is the opposite. He never concentrates; his mind roams outside the farmstead; he cuts corners in all he does, and is unproductive. Naturally, life will be hard for him, for his father will put him under certain restrictions and he will not be happy. Being disapproved of by his father, he now gives vent to his displeasure by his conduct toward his mother. She becomes the target for his surliness and complaints.

All this pictures our attitude to God, both parents representing him. Do we consciously aim to please God, as the ideal son does? Are all our plans and hopes for his glory and service? Whatever happens to us, joy or sorrow, difficulty or ease, our assignment and our delight should be to please God. This is the aim of a wise son. If, however, we do not have this aim, seldom listen to God, rarely applying his Word to our lives, then we will soon lose the evidence of God's blessing toward us. This, in turn, will lead to discontent, and while we may not articulate it our gloomy condition will amount to dissatisfaction with God, and grumbling against him. That is the warning conveyed in this proverb. A wise believer intentionally sets his face to please his heavenly Lord, but a foolish one lives vaguely and becomes discontented.

It is interesting that in this proverb we read in the first line of a 'wise son', and in the second of a 'foolish man'. The second son seems to have been dispossessed, and to have lost his status as a son, and perhaps his inheritance. He is just a 'man'. A true believer cannot lose his salvation, but how tragic if he loses assurance and joy, resembling an unblessed person.

9. Spiritual happiness requires depth

Proverbs 15.21 discloses another important factor in finding spiritual happiness: 'Folly *[literally – silliness]* is joy to him that is destitute of wisdom.' Folly here refers to foolish, trivial, banal, nonsensical things. 'Destitute of wisdom' is 'void of heart' in the Hebrew. To such a person, folly is joy. Or we may turn it around and say, to love trivia and nonsense is to become void of wisdom.

We are children of God, equipped with a new outlook and a new life, but we will quickly surrender spiritual depth and strength by developing a liking for foolish, shallow, and silly things, and being satisfied with them. We must refuse the dumbing down which is all around us in society today. The longer we are believers, the more we are amazed at the shallow pleasures of worldlings. Yet there are Christians who perpetually engage in a sanitised form of empty banter, or endlessly text each other with trivia. We can certainly have light and humorous conversations, but if that is *all* we have, we reduce ourselves, wilfully renouncing God-given intelligence, adopting lightness, and forfeiting all opportunity to handle weightier subjects.

Believers may be light-hearted, but we should never let the trivial and the banal take over entire conversations, because that will diminish and deprive us, making us strangely deformed. We have spiritually enlivened, emancipated minds, that are not fulfilled by playing the part of empty-headed simpletons. What a tragedy when folly becomes our only source of joy! 'A man of understanding *[or discernment]* walketh uprightly,' continues the proverb, denoting the opposite of folly. To have depth, and solid things to say is vital to happiness, because only then are we true to our re-created spiritual nature, whereas to quip and giggle non-stop over petty things is to shrink one's tastes and soul. Let our aim be, humour certainly and a degree of light-heartedness, but chiefly worthy, edifying and productive conversation. Do we make or break our spiritual happiness at this point?

10. Ongoing openness to instruction helps happiness

Similar 'versions' of *Proverbs 15.22* are found elsewhere (at *11.14* and *24.6*), but in each setting there is a different theme. Here, the context is spiritual happiness. 'Without counsel purposes are disappointed: but in the multitude of counsellors they are established.' In *Proverbs 15.20* the father was giving training to his sons, and in verse 21 the education picture continues, for we have one person who loves foolishness, and another who pursues understanding. Verse 22 is another 'education' verse, but now the sons have grown up, and the more adult word for instruction is employed – *counsel.* They are not teenagers any more, or lads undergoing their apprenticeship, but adults, possibly married men. However, says the proverb, they still need education, only now it will be called advice.

So it is with the mature Christian. We are no longer in Sunday School, but we must ever be learning the Word of God, and following its counsels. Without this ongoing learning process, we will prove inadequate before all the wiles of the devil, and our lives will take many wrong directions. 'The multitude of counsellors' in this proverb does not necessarily point to a literal multiplicity of advisers, for it is a picture of the Word of God and its many narratives, principles and sermons. If we seriously study and heed God's Book then our purposes will be established and we shall be stable and instrumental. Surely this will lead to great contentment. Therefore, the ongoing process of learning and applying God's Word in every situation and in every stage of life is the stairway to spiritual happiness.

11. Instrumentality is happiness

Proverbs 15.23 adds an immensely significant factor to the quest for spiritual contentment, reminding us how much joy comes from helping others. 'A man hath joy by the answer of his mouth.' The word translated 'answer' is a Hebrew word that refers not only to a reply, but to our response to any situation. Let us imagine that a man well-versed in all the complexities of agriculture and animal husbandry is called to help a neighbouring farm in serious trouble. He knows exactly how to solve the problem, and gives the very advice that is needed. The proverb speaks of this man's happiness because he is able to help so much by his response. He has responded to desperate need and given great relief, and this makes him very happy. The second part of the proverb seals the interpretation, for – 'a word spoken in due season, how good is it!'

If we learn deeply the things of God and advance, then we can really help others, and this consolidates our own spiritual happiness. We have proved the Lord, and now we give the Gospel to others, and souls are saved. Perhaps, with grace and humility, we shall deliver fellow-believers from many a fall, and we shall certainly spread encouragement. How we shall bless God for instrumentality, and how it will lift up our own spirit!

12. Keeping Heaven in view spurs happiness

Proverbs 15.24 assures us that spiritual happiness also needs a clear view of eternal glory. 'The way of life is above to the wise, that he may depart from hell *[or the grave]* beneath.' We should think often and in some detail of the destination that is ours at the end of life's journey. We remember that God has saved us to be on a heavenly road, consciously heading for that glorious paradise. So frequently this reflection will shrink down all our troubles and problems, enabling us to gain real perspective. A strong anticipation of our destination, and a firm concept of earthly pilgrimage will deliver us from entrapment by this world. It will no longer be 'our place', but a sense of calling and future privilege will hold us and sustain our spiritual joy. The way of life is above, and we look up, and by so doing we are lifted above the purely earthly existence of those whose destiny is no higher than the grave.

13. Spiritual security seals spiritual happiness

Proverbs 15.25 is our final verse in this study on the theme of happiness: 'The Lord will destroy *[the Hebrew says tear down]* the house of the proud: but he will establish the border *[the boundary]* of the widow.' A troubled believer may say: 'Pastor, for all that you've said, my life is very hard, and my situation very difficult. I have great disadvantages that you will not know about, and they weigh down on me all the time.'

It must first be remembered that Christians have always known troubles like this. C. H. Spurgeon, writing about the need for his orphanage, speaks of the grinding poverty suffered by many in Victorian times, none more so than the destitute single parents.

Many Christians have endured really painful poverty. Then there are believers in every age who battle against poor health, as well as those who are sorely persecuted. Numerous believers bear huge burdens and disappointments, and they may say, 'My situation is very, very hard. What can I experience of spiritual happiness?' But this is exactly the situation this proverb addresses.

The first line of the proverb states a well-known fact, but it is stated to strengthen the impact of the second, contrasting line. 'The Lord will destroy the house of the proud.' Self-sufficient people who disdain God and are so very pleased with themselves will find their life one day torn away. But the Lord 'will establish the border of the widow'. Here we are called to imagine a woman who has been left alone in those very difficult and often heartless times. Her husband has died leaving her vulnerable and defenceless. She has her piece of land, but her unscrupulous neighbours may well move her boundary stones, reducing the size of her plot and stealing from her meagre field. This is intended as a picture of how she may be exploited in all manner of ways, because she is unable to defend herself. But, in this proverb, the Lord says, 'I have my eye on my child, a poor widow, and I will protect her boundary stone. I, the living God, will keep her safe.' If we have great problems, we have an omnipotent Lord also. We have a Saviour who went to Calvary and there took away all our sins. We have the righteousness of Christ offered up for us for our eternal security. We have spiritual light, and life, and boundless help. We have so many blessings, and we have a great and glorious God who will maintain us spiritually, keep us close to himself, and jealously guard our lot and our situation. He is pledged to watch over us every day.

We will not need, as it were, CCTV cameras to protect us, scanned from time to time by a fallible person in a remote location. The Lord will watch our boundary stone every minute of every day, and, in the word of the proverb, he will *establish* it, root it deeply in the ground. This is about wonderful security. Even if our problems are so great that we quake within, we must remember that the Lord is the special defender of those who are vulnerable and exposed to hardship and difficulty. We will read *Romans 8.18-39* often and prayerfully, for these verses are nothing other than the New Testament amplification of this glorious proverb. It is all about spiritual joy and happiness, for this is grounded in the sense of security that flows from the promises of God valued and remembered.

* * *

This group of proverbs tells us, first, that we have a duty to feel contentment and happiness in the Lord (achieved by reflection and praise). We are also to feed our minds on deep and worthy things in order to be able to stand up to trials when they come. Misery or joyfulness, we learn, are continuous prevailing moods, and we must seek to make happiness our prevailing, underlying characteristic. Then we must never let earthly aims and delights, however legitimate, overtake our love and commitment to Christ, for he must be first. An angry, murmuring spirit, we are taught, undermines communion with God and therefore spiritual happiness, and so does laziness in spiritual duties. We must consciously do everything we do to please God, and never allow ourselves to wallow in trivial things. We must continue, even as spiritual 'adults', to faithfully consult the Bible in every situation and project, and, because much happiness comes by fruitfulness, we must be useful to others. It is essential that we take an eternal view of life, reflecting on and rejoicing in our glorious destination, and finally, we should never forget the widow's boundary stone – the assurance that God will keep us spiritually safe right to the end. All these steps or duties for happiness deserve deeper study, but this is the counsel of a precious group of proverbs. May the happiness purchased for us on Calvary by the eternal Son of God be possessed and enjoyed by us, leading to his praise and honour and glory through the prevailing disposition of our lives.

10
Walking in the Spirit

'And I will pray the Father, and he shall give you another Comforter, that he may abide with you for ever' *(John 14.16).*

THERE IS A WEALTH of teaching in the Scripture about the Holy Spirit, but this chapter will be confined to the promises of Christ in *John 14-15* that were given to the future apostles as they trained at his feet. Few subjects can be so central to the Christian life and so vital to us.

1. The Spirit as Comforter

We will draw from six glorious aspects of the Spirit's work, considering first the word 'Comforter' in *John 14.16*, 'I will pray the Father, and he shall give you another Comforter.' Why is the Greek translated in our *King James Version* as 'Comforter' (following Tyndale), when most of the modern versions have 'helper' or even 'advocate'? Those words are a valid way of translating the original, but earlier translators clearly adopted the option 'Comforter' because of the context.

The introductory words to the passage are about the disciples' hearts being concerned because Christ is going away: 'Let not your heart be troubled: ye believe in God, believe also in me.' Similarly at the end of this passage we read – 'Let not your heart be troubled, neither let it be afraid.' And in verse 18 the sentiment occurs again, 'I will not leave you comfortless *[orphaned].*' So the earlier translators, considering the context, chose to use the word 'Comforter'.

The particular work of the Spirit focused on here is the comfort and the assurance of the Holy Spirit. The Saviour spoke of 'another Comforter', because, of course, Christ was already their Comforter. The Holy Spirit will be 'another' such, taking up the role of Christ. The Lord himself was their first counsellor, guide, protector, teacher, and inspiration, but the Holy Spirit would take over these roles in his absence, and would abide with Christ's people 'for ever', throughout the last phase of this world's existence before the Lord returns.

He is our Comforter when the adversary strikes with depressing, doubting ideas, or by stirring up opposition and slanders. We pray, and reflect on our calling and Christ's love, and the Holy Spirit applies those blessings to our hearts with inexplicable power, and we are lifted up. He is our Comforter when a very great loss, or a time of sickness or a grievous disappointment presses us down, and we call out to God, and the Spirit unmistakably bears us through with a strength unknown before. He is our Comforter when a season of seeming barrenness falls on us, when instrumentality fails and impenetrable gloom surrounds us, and we pray, and the Spirit enables us suddenly to see the hand of God at work in ways we had not perceived. The Holy Spirit in so many ways is our ever-generous, almighty, unfailing Comforter.

The very same Comforter that preserved and enlivened the apostles through all their persecution, and who upheld the Luthers and the Whitefields and the Spurgeons down the rolling centuries, is the Comforter of every child of God.

2. The Spirit of truth

Three times the Lord Jesus Christ called the Holy Spirit 'the Spirit of truth' *(John 14.17; 15.26; 16.13)*. We know that he possesses and shares all the attributes of God, with the Father and the Son. He is eternal, infinite, holy, all-powerful, all-knowing, and all-wise, as they also are, so why does the Saviour particularly single out *truth*? Because in every sense he promotes the truth as far as the true church is concerned. The Old Testament church, the Jewish church, the *typical* church – that phase of God's redemptive work, was not entirely true, realistic or genuine because it consisted of saints and sinners mixed together. The majority, at most times, appear to have been unsaved, unconverted. We read of many through the Old Testament who were saved, indeed who were heroes of faith, but Israel was nevertheless a mixed entity. Believing New Testament churches, however, are characterised by truth, that is, they are true congregations of regenerate people that seek to maintain, as far as is humanly, reasonably possible, a saved membership *(Jeremiah 31.33-34)*. No longer is it saints and sinners mixed together, a minority of believers and a majority of nominal believers who have no true hold upon God. The Holy Spirit will be in charge of believing churches, and he will work to ensure their purity. He is the Spirit of truth, of reality, and of genuineness, and these should be hallmarks of a Christian church, as well as of Christian character.

The Holy Spirit is also the Spirit of truth in that he reveals truth, the Word of God. The future apostles along with selected prophets would be inspired to write Scripture – the New Testament – according to Christ's words: 'The Spirit of truth ... he will guide you into all truth' *(John 16.13)*. It is Christ's Word, given to them by the inspiration of the Spirit, and so is the entire Bible, a revelation having a single author – the Holy Spirit. Both Old and New Testaments must be understood and interpreted by the rules the Bible itself teaches, such as the comparing of scripture with scripture

(1 Corinthians 2.13), and, of course, through prayer for the help of the Holy Spirit himself.

When you look at today's Bible-believing church scene, you see many churches whose doctrines are inconsistent, and some who show little interest in being consistent. But the Holy Spirit's work is to bring us to grasp the teachings of God without having ideas that contradict Scripture and each other. He is the Spirit of *truth* and he deepens us in truth. We have observed already the existence of the counselling movement, which borrows heavily from atheistic secular counselling, mixing it with elements of Christian truth. But the Spirit will not bless this confusion of light and darkness, because he is the Spirit of truth.

As a youngster this writer was surprised to discover how the Puritans approached the counselling ministry. Reading a Puritan author, Thomas Boston, in a famous book entitled, *The Crook in the Lot*, I saw how he set out to comfort believers in various troubles and doubts. The subtitle was – 'The Sovereignty and Wisdom of God, in the Afflictions of Men Displayed', and the book focused entirely on doctrinal teaching. Thomas Boston knew that this is the only *true* comfort for Christians – believing the doctrines and promises of God, and putting their trust in them. That is how most past preachers and teachers went about giving comfort. Now, many prefer to borrow from the secular world, but the Spirit is the Holy Spirit of truth, and that is what he will use and bless.

John Newton penned hymns in this very spirit, directing minds to the power and love of God, and urging us to faith.

> *Brought safely by his hand thus far,*
> *Why should I now give place to fear?*
> *How can I want if he provide,*
> *Or lose my way with such a Guide?*

---

* For a treatment of the steps of interpretation of the Bible, see *Not Like Any Other Book*, by Peter Masters, published by Wakeman Trust.

When first before his mercy-seat
My all to him I did commit,
He gave me warrant from that hour
To trust his wisdom, love and power.

I remember years ago visiting a believer in hospital and there happened to be a man in the next bed clearly dying. His relatives were round the bed saying to him, 'You are going to get better, Dad; you are going to get better. You will be out of here in no time.' It was just not true. If only he had been able to receive spiritual light and comfort, there would have been *truth* in their encounter. They could have spoken about future glory, and praised God for having led their father to true salvation. All the best comforts are essentially doctrinal and they are administered to the soul by the Holy Spirit, who cannot be involved in untruths.

3. The Spirit of communion

In speaking of the Holy Spirit, the Lord told the disciples – 'But ye know him; for he dwelleth with you, and shall be in you. I will not leave you comfortless: I will come to you' *(John 14.17-18)*. Although it is true that the Lord did come to them himself in the resurrection appearances, he seems here to refer to his coming by the provision of the Holy Spirit. Christ will be represented by the Holy Spirit. A little later he would say, 'I tell you the truth; it is expedient for you that I go away: for if I go not away, the Comforter will not come unto you; but if I depart, I will send him unto you' *(John 16.7)*.

The Holy Spirit cannot come until Christ has gone to Heaven, after Calvary, after the great redemptive act, and once the disciples are left alone to know the Saviour by faith, not by sight. And it will be, says the Lord, to their advantage that the Comforter comes. We wonder how having the Holy Spirit, who is invisible to us, can be better than having the presence of Christ. Who could be better than Christ? The answer is plain. When Christ was on earth, he was bound to live in a human body and voluntarily confine himself to human limitations in many ways. He was still God, knowing all things even as he wore human nature, and doing great works exhibiting divine power. But in his physical body if he was in one place, he could not be elsewhere at the same time. Only a small band of disciples around could see him close up, feel his touch, hear his words and know his direct influences. He could not, in his human body, be with believers in all places at the same time. So of course it is immensely to the advantage of believers that when Christ went, the Holy Spirit came, not confined to a body, able to indwell and deal with us all, directly. We may expand the promise of the Lord: 'But ye know him; for he dwelleth with you [all believers, wherever you are, all the time], and shall be in you. I will not leave you comfortless: I will come to you.'

The Holy Spirit indwells every believing heart to perform the same role that Christ exercised toward his intimate disciples when he was on earth. By the Spirit we know closeness with God, and the Spirit stirs our consciences when temptation attacks, and often prompts and urges us to acts of Christian duty or witness or compassion, and imparts strength and comfort whenever we call upon him.

The Holy Spirit will not reveal to us new revelation outside his Word, as charismatic teachers so often claim, being ignorant of the Scripture, because revelation is complete. As far as new truth is concerned the canon of Scripture is closed. But he will frequently bring scriptures and biblical principles that we have learned into our memories as he urges and prompts us in our spiritual walk.

It is the Holy Spirit who gives us that indescribable sense of audience with God when we pray. Who can explain the quiet assurance and certainty that surrounds us so frequently in devotions, or the sense of being heard, of being 'family', and the times of peace following prayer, as though we have been divested of a heavy burden? It is the Holy Spirit who gives us a taste of divine love, of being in the Lord's sight, and in his care, and in his purpose. It is the Spirit who grants the sense of sin taken away, of love for the Word, and of praise and thanksgiving. The Holy Spirit is the sharing Spirit, who gives the certainty of being partakers in the vast work of redemption, and participants in the eternal heavenly choir of those who adore the Saviour. We read of Christ that – 'before the feast of the passover, when Jesus knew that his hour was come that he should depart out of this world unto the Father, having loved his own which were in the world, he loved them unto the end.' The Holy Spirit expresses that same love as our guardian and indwelling God. It is our enjoyment of such love that forms and nourishes distinctive Christian character.

4. The Spirit of holiness

We also read of the Holy Spirit, 'the Comforter, which is the *Holy Ghost*'. The holiness of the Spirit is to be especially emphasised. We do not think enough about the fact that he is with us to advance our holiness and purity. It is wonderful to have the Spirit of truth deepening our sincerity and genuineness, and to have his companionship, closeness, strength and promptings, but we must also have him as our Spirit of holiness.

Here is a daunting illustration. Supposing we had assigned to our home a team of supercleaners who did nothing but frenetically wash and clean everything all day, round the clock. Our job would be to dispose of the rubbish and strip out any clutter that stands in their way, and their job is to clean. They also have authority to reprove us if we leave rubbish around, or anything that obstructs their work. The thought is frightening, and a poor illustration, but may help us to think rightly when we consider the Holy Spirit.

We have as our divine resident one who is with us for cleanliness and purity, and we must co-operate. Are we slovenly, spiritually speaking? Do we leave unconfessed, undealt-with sin in the house of our soul, along with unaddressed faults and failings? Do we not mind these polluting things? Is our spiritual house full of inappropriate matter, perhaps foul secret sins, and we have not shown any concern to clear them out?

How much more conscientious we need to be about holiness! When the Holy Spirit engages the conscience over something that we are about to say or do, we must listen and heed. If we ignore or regard as inconvenient the Spirit's promptings of conscience, pressing ahead to say or do sinful things regardless, we push aside the Spirit of God and risk grieving him away.

The indwelling of the Holy Spirit has wonderful aspects such as comfort and strengthening, illumination and teaching, but we cannot choose to accept some of his activities without others. He is the Spirit of *holiness*, and we must be deeply serious about daily self-examination, repentance and the re-pledging of ourselves to him.

With the ongoing privilege of divine residency comes a deep responsibility. Do old sins come back barely noticed? Are we really conscientious about the walk of righteousness? Do we co-operate with the work of the Spirit? Responsiveness to the sanctifying work of the Spirit is a hallmark of Christian character.

5. The Spirit of illumination

We return to the words of *John 14.26*: 'But the Comforter, which is the Holy Ghost, whom the Father will send in my name, he shall teach you all things, and bring all things to your remembrance, whatsoever I have said unto you.'

As we have seen, these words applied first and foremost to the apostles themselves, to whom the Spirit would give a clear recollection of all things that Christ said and did in his earthly ministry. Some of them were to be penmen of Holy Scripture, writers of the Gospel record and of epistles also. Others would authenticate the inspired words of New Testament prophets. What they wrote or attested would bring Scripture to completion, so that there would be nothing further to reveal.

So the Lord's words applied first to the apostles, but secondarily they apply to believers in every day and age, all who believingly read the Word. When we read the Scripture, praying for the help of the Spirit, we are helped and enabled to grasp the message of the passage so that it shapes our conduct and thinking. It is a good practice to read the Word with key questions in our minds. We first take in the plain sense and obvious significance, but then we look again and apply our devotional questions, such as: What sight of my Saviour do I have in this passage? What reproof is there to me? What encouragement, or what instruction, or what duty do I see? Is there a message here about the church? Do I see any particular doctrine here? Is there a comfort or a promise for this very day? To search the passage in this way is so valuable, and the Holy Spirit opens our eyes as we do so.

Returning to the words of Christ about the Spirit bringing all things to remembrance, this promise has special value to us in an age crowded with information. Perhaps you are witnessing to someone and the very moment you wish to quote a key text, you find it has fled from your mind, and your line of reasoning flounders. But if you depend upon the Spirit of God, pray for help and proceed in trust and dependence, he will even help you to remember those scriptures. He brings to our remembrance his own Word, and many believers will testify to this.

6. The Spirit of testimony

In *John 15.26* we read – 'But when the Comforter is come…he shall testify of me.' The word 'testify' means he will *bear witness* regarding Christ. It is the Spirit who illuminates hearts, bringing lost souls to recognise that the Word is divine truth, and enabling them to understand and believe it. The Holy Spirit is the power in all our witness and evangelism, for he is the Spirit of testimony. The Lord Jesus Christ goes on to say: 'And ye also shall bear witness, because ye have been with me from the beginning' *(John 15.27)*. We also are commissioned to be witnesses.

When a preacher preaches an evangelistic sermon, his desire is that the Holy Spirit will use him to witness to Christ. He must make sure that Christ is in his message, and that his glories and love and work on Calvary are plainly visible. You cannot have an evangelistic sermon (that the Spirit will use) without Christ and without Calvary, for the Spirit's supreme delight is to witness to him.

Equally in the everyday life of the Christian, the Holy Spirit inspires and empowers witness to the Saviour. We have him as Comforter, illuminator of the Word, provider of communion and sanctifying power, but we sometimes shun him as the Spirit of testimony, choosing to remain silent rather than speak a word in season. 'Quench not the Spirit,' says Paul in *1 Thessalonians 5.19*. What blessing and instrumentality is lost because the Holy Spirit's highest role in us is stifled.

In the middle of *John 16.13* there is a tremendously important phrase in Christ's teaching about the role and work of the Spirit – 'for he shall not speak of himself.' Over the years exegetes have tried to describe the stance or manner of the Holy Spirit in this respect and found it extremely difficult to express. He has been called the 'reserved' Spirit. Here the Spirit is seen as reserved, shy, quiet, and remaining in the background. He has infinite power to bend hearts and wills, and speaks of Christ, magnifying him, but never exalts himself. He has also been called the 'retiring' Spirit, to show how he keeps in the background and exalts Christ and not himself. He has been called the 'reticent' Holy Spirit, holding back the manifestation of his glorious being in order that he may honour Christ. He has been called the 'unostentatious' Holy Spirit, unobtrusive, withdrawn. All these terms express something of the truth. The Holy Spirit does not magnify himself.

One of the mistakes of Pentecostalism (even at its most earnest) is the failure to understand the retiring, unostentatious Spirit. They seem to want to exhibit the Holy Spirit like a placard carried at the head of a procession as if to say, 'We will show you the Spirit.' Of course we must teach the doctrine of the Holy Spirit, believing that only he can do the work of God for us and through us, and we must depend entirely upon him. But he works to help us to magnify Christ, and not, according to the Saviour, to make a great show of himself. We depend upon him with all our hearts, and endeavour not to grieve him, and the more we lift up Christ in the world, the greater will be the blessing of the Spirit upon us.

* * *

We have considered in this chapter the Spirit of comfort, of truth, of sincerity, of genuineness, of communion and of holiness, with whom we must co-operate. We have considered also the Spirit of illumination and of witness. We have acknowledged that we must have him in all his offices and objectives. We cannot leave off, say, the witness, or the holiness, or dependence upon him for illumination. We need him for a sense of communion, and he is the one who prompts and urges us by the operation of conscience and the inspiring of godly action. How much we need and value and desire every gracious operation of the Holy Spirit in our lives. With him and by him we are wholly yielded up to the Lord, and bear the marks of spiritual character.

The Personal Spiritual Life
127 pages, paperback, ISBN 978 1 908919 20 5

From the personal indwelling of the Holy Spirit to living a life of commitment these chapters stir and encourage readers to advance spiritually.

In what sense may we 'feel' the presence of the Lord? What was the apostle Paul's method for progress in holiness? How may we identify our spiritual gifts? And how may we count more for the Lord, and sustain spiritual joy?

These are among the themes of this tonic for present-day disciples of Christ.

The Lord's Pattern for Prayer
118 pages, paperback, ISBN 978 1 870855 36 5

Subtitled – 'Studying the lessons and spiritual encouragements in the most famous of all prayers.' This volume is almost a manual on prayer, providing a real spur to the devotional life. The Lord's own plan and agenda for prayer – carefully amplified – takes us into the presence of the Father, to prove the privileges and power of God's promises to those who pray.

Chapters cover each petition in the Lord's Prayer. Here, too, are sections on remedies for problems in prayer, how to intercede for others, the reasons why God keeps us waiting for answers, and the nature of the prayer of faith.

God's Rules for Holiness
Unlocking the Ten Commandments
139 pages, paperback, ISBN 978 1 870855 37 2

Taken at face value the Ten Commandments are binding on all people, and will guard the way to Heaven, so that evil will never spoil its glory and purity. But the Commandments are far greater than their surface meaning, as this book shows.

They challenge us as Christians on a still wider range of sinful deeds and attitudes. They provide positive virtues as goals. And they give immense help for staying close to the Lord in our walk and worship.

The Commandments are vital for godly living and for greater blessing, but we need to enter into the panoramic view they provide for the standards and goals for redeemed people.

Faith, Doubts, Trials and Assurance
139 pages, paperback, ISBN 978 1 870855 50 1

Ongoing faith is essential for answered prayer, effective service, spiritual stability and real communion with God. In this book many questions are answered about faith, such as – How may we assess the state of our faith? How can faith be strengthened? What are the most dangerous doubts? How should difficult doubts be handled? What is the biblical attitude to trials? How can we tell if troubles are intended to chastise or to refine? What can be done to obtain assurance? What are the sources of assurance? Can a believer commit the unpardonable sin? Exactly how is the Lord's presence felt?

Dr Masters provides answers, with much pastoral advice, drawing on Scripture throughout.

Steps for Guidance
In the Journey of Life
134 pages, paperback, ISBN 978 1 870855 66 2

In recent years the subject of how to find God's guidance has become controversial. Some say that God does not have a specific plan for the lives of his people, but allows us to please ourselves. Others say God's will is known by dreams, visions, and 'words of knowledge'.

By contrast with these sadly unbiblical ideas, this book presents the time-honoured, scriptural view that Christians must seek God's will in all the major decisions of life, such as career, marriage, location, and church. Six essential steps are traced from the Bible, and principles are given on additional practical issues such as possessions and leisure activities; ambition and wealth; joining or leaving a church.

Here is a strong challenge to authentic Christian commitment, with an abundance of pastoral advice.

Church Membership in the Bible
61 pages, paperback, ISBN 978 1 870855 64 8

Christ has designed a 'home' or family for his people, described in these pages as an accomplishment of divine genius. This is a magnificent subject, vital to spiritual growth and blessing and also to our service for the Saviour.

This book answers many questions about churches and church membership in New Testament times. Next to having a real walk with Christ and knowing the doctrines of the faith, membership of a good church has a powerful formative influence on the believer's life.

The Faith
Great Christian Truths
119 pages, paperback, ISBN 978 1 870855 54 9

There is nothing like this popular, non-technical sweep through key themes of the Christian faith, highlighting very many inspiring and enlivening points. It often takes an unusual approach to a topic in order to bring out the full wonder and significance. It is designed to be enjoyed by seasoned Christians, and also by all who want to explore the great features of the faith, and discover the life of the soul.

CONTENTS:

The Mysterious Nature of a Soul	The New Birth
What God is Actually Like	Why the Resurrection?
The Fall of Man	Prophecies of Resurrection
The Three Dark Hours of Calvary	The Holy Trinity

Not Like Any Other Book
Interpreting the Bible
161 pages, paperback, ISBN 978 1 870855 43 3

Faulty Bible interpretation lies at the root of every major mistake and 'ism' assailing churches today, and countless Christians are asking for the old, traditional and proven way of handling the Bible to be spelled out plainly.

A new approach to interpretation has also gripped many evangelical seminaries and Bible colleges, an approach based on the ideas of unbelieving critics, stripping the Bible of God's message, and leaving pastors impoverished in their preaching.

This book reveals what is happening, providing many brief examples of right and wrong interpretation. The author shows that the Bible includes its own rules of interpretation, and every believer should know what these are.

Do We Have a Policy?
Paul's Ten Point Policy for Church Health & Growth
93 pages, paperback, ISBN 978 1 870855 30 3

What are our aims for the shaping of our church fellowship, and for its growth? Do we have an agenda or framework of desired objectives? The apostle Paul had a very definite policy, and called it his 'purpose', using a Greek word which means – a plan or strategy displayed for all to see.

This book sets out ten policy ideals, gleaned from Paul's teaching, all of which are essential for the health and growth of a congregation today.

Worship in the Melting Pot

148 pages, paperback, ISBN 978 1 870855 33 4

'Worship is truly in the melting pot,' says the author. 'A new style of praise has swept into evangelical life shaking to the foundations traditional concepts and attitudes.' How should we react? Is it all just a matter of taste and age? Will churches be helped, or changed beyond recognition?

This book presents four essential principles which Jesus Christ laid down for worship, and by which every new idea must be judged.

Here also is a fascinating view of how they worshipped in Bible times, including their rules for the use of instruments, and the question is answered – What does the Bible teach about the content and order of a service of worship today?

Physicians of Souls
The Gospel Ministry

285 pages, paperback, ISBN 978 1 870855 34 1

'Compelling, convicting, persuasive preaching, revealing God's mercy and redemption to dying souls, is seldom heard today. The noblest art ever granted to our fallen human race has almost disappeared.'

Even where the free offer of the Gospel is treasured in principle, regular evangelistic preaching has become a rarity, contends the author. These pages tackle the inhibitions, theological and practical, and provide powerful encouragement for physicians of souls to preach the Gospel. A vital anatomy or order of conversion is supplied with advice for counselling seekers.

The author shows how passages for evangelistic persuasion may be selected and prepared. He also challenges modern church growth techniques, showing the superiority of direct proclamation. These and other key topics make up a complete guide to soulwinning.

The Baptist Confession of Faith 1689
Edited by Peter Masters
53 pages, paperback, ISBN 978 1 870855 24 2

C. H. Spurgeon said of this great Confession – 'Here the youngest members of our church will have a body of Truth in small compass, and by means of the scriptural proofs, will be able to give a reason of the hope that is in them.' This brilliant summary of doctrine (in the same family as the Westminster Confession), with its invaluable proof texts, is here gently modernised in punctuation, with archaic words replaced. Explanations of difficult phrases have been added in italic brackets. A brief history of the Confession, with an index, is included.

The Charismatic Illusion

Co-author: John C. Whitcomb

100 pages, paperback, ISBN 978 1 908919 70 0

Now with more answers to questions asked by people investigating the arguments, this veteran book contends for the biblical position on the gifts that prevailed for nearly 2,000 years before the charismatic movement came along.

Here is the dynamic teaching of the Spirit that sustained true churches and believers through dark and bright years of history, through the Reformation, through the Puritan era, through the time of great Confessions of Faith, through repeated awakenings and revivals, and through the worldwide growth of the modern missionary movement.

Here is the case for authentic biblical spiritual life.

The Healing Epidemic

143 pages, paperback, ISBN 978 1 908919 24 3

Dr Masters here answers the arguments used by healers in support of their methods. He explains Bible teaching on what demons can and cannot do, and how *James 5* should be implemented in churches today. He also proves that the conscious mind should always be switched on for spiritual activities. Included is a brilliant assessment of miraculous healing by a leading British medical professor.

'This volume is a masterful analysis and criticism of the most recent manifestations of charismatic phenomena . . . The exposition of *James 5.13-14* is excellent, and his analysis of the place of the mind in the Christian's experience is remarkable.' – Bibliotheca Sacra

Only One Baptism of the Holy Spirit

109 pages, paperback, ISBN 978 1 870855 17 4

Young Christians these days are confronted by much confusion on the teaching of the Holy Spirit and how he baptises, fills and anoints God's people. Contradictory statements and clashing ideas flow from a new generation of anecdotal-style books.

When is the believer baptized with the Spirit, and what does it amount to? Is there a second baptism? How exactly does the Spirit witness with our spirit? How does assurance come? Is the believer to struggle against sin, or does the Lord fight the battle for him? What is the filling of the Spirit? Clear answers are given to all such questions, with 'proof texts'. Ideal for all, especially young believers and study groups.

Joshua's Conquest
Was it Moral? What Does It Say to Us Today?
119 pages, paperback, ISBN 978 1 870855 46 4

This is a book for reading, rather than a commentary. Its aim is to bring out the spiritual message of the *Book of Joshua* for today, and also to explain some of the 'problem' portions and passages which evoke questions on, for example, the morality of so much killing, and whether God was responsible for hardening the hearts of the Canaanites.

The Mutual Love of Christ & His People
An explanation of the *Song of Solomon* for personal devotions and Bible study groups
115 pages, paperback, ISBN 978 1 870855 40 2

The courtship of the *Song of Solomon* provides fascinating scenes and events designed to show the love of Christ for his redeemed people, and theirs for him. Prophecies of Christ abound. Here, also, are lessons for Christians when they become cold or backslidden, showing the way to recover Christ's presence in their lives.

Biblical Strategies for Witness
154 pages, paperback, ISBN 978 1 870855 18 1

It is not widely realised just how much practical guidance is stored in the Gospels and the *Book of Acts* for all who engage in personal witness and preaching. Are we aware, for example, that the Lord Jesus Christ employed distinctive strategies for different kinds of unbeliever, and that these may be learned and copied? This study brings these approaches to life for witnessing Christians and preachers today.

Heritage of Evidence
127 pages, 135 colour illustrations, paperback, ISBN 978 1 908919 71 7

The British Museum holds a huge number of major discoveries that provide direct corroboration and background confirmation for an immense sweep of Bible history. This illustrated survey of Bible-authenticating exhibits has been designed as a guide for visitors, and also to give pleasure and interest to readers unable to tour the galleries.

The Dark Side of Christian Counselling
E. S. Williams
155 pages, paperback, ISBN 978 1 870855 65 5

It is amazing how rapidly the Christian counselling movement has spread through churches in the UK, teaching that hurts and depressions once considered part of normal life are illnesses to be treated. It implies that for 1900 years the Bible has been insufficient for the woes of God's people, or for their sanctification, but that now we have the 'insights' of anti-Christian psychologists to make good the deficit.

In this book medical doctor Ted Williams challenges these claims, giving a clear-cut and interesting overview of the counselling movement.

His survey of the careers and teaching of the giants of secular psychology, the pillars of its 'faith', is unique. Nowhere else are these great names so clearly critiqued from a Christian point of view, and their militant atheism laid bare. Yet these are the heroes of the new Christian counselling.

Christ or Therapy?
E. S. Williams
157 pages, paperback, ISBN 978 1 870855 71 6

It is not widely realised that there is an irreconcilable difference between the remedies for sadness and grief set out in the Bible, and those put forward by the world of psychotherapy. A gulf also exists between the biblical policy for marriage, and that proposed by secular marriage guidance psychologists. Many well-known evangelical authors and churches, however, have turned entirely to the secular remedies and policies in these matters. This book shows what the differences are, including a remarkable review of depression in the Bible, and its relief.

This is the sequel to *The Dark Side of Christian Counselling*.

For a full listing of Wakeman titles please see www.wakemantrust.org